"A groundbreaking work about a sacramen[t] yet whose theology and practice are often d[...]. The author's modest and respectful tone bel[...] [...]mance and depth of this book. Both pastorally poignant and pertinent, this is a must read for pastoral ministers interested in deepening their appreciation of what is often a misunderstood sacrament."

—Rev. Msgr. Kevin Irwin
Ordinary Professor of Liturgical Studies and Sacramental Theology
The Msgr. Walter J. Schmitz, S. S. Professor of Liturgical Studies
The Catholic University of America

"Timothy Gabrielli's study of confirmation and U.S. culture in the twentieth century is a welcome addition to the literature on this sacrament 'in search of a theology.' This book explains why we think about confirmation in the different ways that we do and it encourages those charged with preparing others for this sacrament always to keep in mind that the Catholic faith and its sacramental practices occur in a cultural context that always has an impact on how the Gospel is understood and lived. I highly recommend this book for religious educators or anyone who wants a deeper understanding of the interplay between culture and sacramental theology/practice."

—Timothy Brunk
Associate Professor of Theology
Villanova University

"Timothy Gabrielli jumps with both feet into the 'ongoing conversation' about the meaning of Confirmation. . . . He writes clearly and insightfully. As one who has participated actively in this conversation for several decades, I recommend this book to all who play a role in helping young Catholics to develop and deepen a relationship with the indwelling Person of the Holy Spirit."

—Sister Kieran Sawyer, SSND
Confirming Faith, Ave Maria Press

"Anyone discussing confirmation must bring to the conversation hefty amounts of courage and wisdom, and Timothy Gabrielli does bring both. His survey of theological, psychological, charismatic, and humanist motifs—which, since Pius X's 1910 *Quam Singulari*, have been used to explain the meaning of confirmation—highlights how different understandings of the sacrament have been influenced by the evolving relationship of Catholics to the American culture. Emphasizing that confirmation confers the gift of the Person of the Holy Spirit, *Confirmation: How a Sacrament of God's Grace Became All about Us* is a worthy contribution to our study of the sacrament many consider still to be 'in search of a theology.'"

> —Fr. Kurt Stasiak, OSB
> Professor of Sacramental-Liturgical Theology
> Saint Meinrad Seminary

"Timothy Gabrielli is to be commended for having navigated with great balance and skill the complexities regarding the theology and practice of the Sacrament of Confirmation, positing his exploration within the increasingly diverse cultural reality that is the twenty-first century Church in North America. The historical, theological, and pastoral depth of this work, written in a clear and accessible style, will make this book a very useful resource for scholars and pastoral practitioners alike."

> —Keith F. Pecklers, S.J.
> Pontifical Gregorian University
> Pontifical Liturgical Institute
> Rome, Italy

Confirmation

*How a Sacrament of God's Grace
Became All about Us*

Timothy R. Gabrielli

LITURGICAL PRESS
Collegeville, Minnesota

www.litpress.org

1   2   3   4   5   6   7   8   9

Library of Congress Cataloging-in-Publication Data

Gabrielli, Timothy R., 1982–
    Confirmation : how a sacrament of God's grace became all about us / by Timothy Gabrielli.
        pages   cm
    Includes bibliographical references.
    ISBN 978-0-8146-3522-3 — ISBN 978-0-8146-3547-6 (ebook)
    1. Confirmation—Catholic Church—History—20th century.   2. Catholic Church—United States—History—20th century.   I. Title.

BX2210.G33 2013
265'.2—dc23   2013018361

Dedicated to

My mother, Amy Gabrielli (1955–1998),

who saw to it that I was formed in the womb of the church

&

To my daughters, Sofia and Lidia Gabrielli,

may you be continually formed in its womb

Contents

Foreword

Confirmation, according to a classic strain of Catholic tradition, is the sacrament that both signifies and effects a grace-filled strengthening by the Holy Spirit.

Tim Gabrielli has written a book that explores the meaning and practice of this sacrament in twentieth-century United States as well as today. Such an exploration, Gabrielli explains, requires also a simultaneous exploration of how Catholics have experienced the relationship between their faith and the U.S. culture. One cannot understand the first without simultaneously understanding the second. Gabrielli articulates a sophisticated but accessible narrative as he analyzes various catechetical and liturgical approaches to what some have called "the sacrament of choice" and what others have called "the sacrament of exit."

Is the book primarily a history? Is it primarily a systematic theology? Is it primarily a guide for thought for pastoral ministers? Yes. Yes. And Yes.

Gabrielli belongs to a generation of young Catholic theologians who want to get beyond various divisions and to offer intellectual support for the everyday living of the faith. He transcends these divisions not by ignoring them but by understanding them within their own historical context. His book offers an integrated vision of the history, theology, and practice of confirmation. He approaches his subject descriptively and even-handedly, though he also issues clear criticisms as he points to the strengths and weaknesses of a wide variety of positions.

Paradoxically, confirmation had become the sacrament of engagement with the world before that famous council made engagement with the world a key Catholic theme. Paradoxically, a strong focus on engagement with the world has encountered the danger of becoming swallowed up in a culture that somehow manages to overvalue (or perhaps to improperly define) the extremely valuable human capacity for individuality and autonomy. In the end, concerning questions such as the most proper mode of theological understanding for confirmation, or the appropriate age of reception, or the ordering within the sacraments, Gabrielli does not offer one fixed position that would simply take its place along the spectrum of warring factions. Instead, he offers wisdom designed to lead us beyond the polarized camps as we struggle to live out the meaning of the sacraments.

Dennis M. Doyle
University of Dayton
April 14, 2013

Acknowledgments

In one of its many meanings, to confirm something is to lend support to it. *Confirmation* would not be possible without quite a bit of support! Indeed, it is remarkable that such a short book could rest on the hard work of so many, without whom it likely would not have seen the light of day. The following people are some of those who have so worked on its behalf.

Dennis Doyle, who helped to see this project through from its infancy. His patience, wisdom, and prodding were invaluable to me.

Kelly Johnson, who read the manuscript and exercised much grace and charity in discussing its contents with me; William Portier, who also read the manuscript, made helpful suggestions, and offered many exhortations along the way; Sandra Yocum, who provided encouragement as well as a particular insight about Catholic Action literature; Tim Brunk, who without my asking (!) read the entire manuscript and commented; Deb Wilson, who consistently reminded me of the importance of this work for those working in confirmation prep; numerous theologians and diocesan directors of religious education, who provided me with syllabi and information regarding confirmation in their dioceses, respectively; Janet Benestad, who gave me the opportunity to teach teens in the diocese of Scranton; Michael Lombardo, who listened to many a germinating idea, offered incisive comments and much support.

The kind and excellently competent editorial staff at Liturgical Press, who saw the potential of the manuscript and shepherded it to print.

My father and sister, who offered consistent enthusiasm for my work. My brother, Karan Singh, who kept me inspired over numerous cups of coffee and lots of delicious food.

Most importantly, my wife, Jessica, whose love, patience, insight, commitment, and joy constitute a daily gift to me.

Introduction

My interest in the sacrament of confirmation began while teaching religious education for postconfirmation Catholics in the Diocese of Scranton, Pennsylvania from 2001 to 2004. This diocesan-centered program was inaugurated because of a shortage of parish-level postconfirmation catechetical and general religious education programs. In many of the diocese's parishes young people were deprived of ongoing religious education after confirmation. As far as I know the diocese had no centralized mandate regarding the age of confirmation's celebration, but most of the students who entered this program were in grades seven through twelve, so it is safe to assume that confirmation was often celebrated in early adolescence. My colleagues and I taught the students everything from the Pauline Epistles to the Christian tradition of prayer.

There was, however, seemingly constant pastoral strife over the students' involvement with the program. While the diocesan central offices kept trying to drum up support for the program, some pastors were reluctant to recommend their young people because such a recommendation seemed effectively to serve as an indictment of their own failure at the parish level. It seemed, however, that what failed at the parish level was widespread interest from Catholic young people: even parishes that tried to get a program off of the ground were unable to do so because of lack of student interest. The same fate befell the diocesan program: funding was cut off after the numbers failed to increase over several years.

Aside from diocesan politics, there seemed to be a deeper issue here that gave rise to a series of questions. Questions such as: What is it that is so challenging about continuing religious education for teens? Why is it that confirmation serves as a fulcrum for participation in religious education—that is, it is the moment when things seem to change for youth involvement in parish life? Are there theological factors that have contributed to this particular educational phenomenon? What are we doing when we confirm people in adolescence?

These questions and others regarding pneumatology and sacramental theology drove my initial interest in this project in which I had hoped to find the problem and offer a solution. My naïveté was broken by the spectrum of interesting developments of confirmation in twentieth-century America alone. As I dove into the research, I began to discover that confirmation stood as a symbol, a flagship, a cornerstone, a mode of appeal, and a sacramental legitimation of various movements and renewals central to the development of Catholicism in the United States during the last century.

Further research on this particular score led me to the thesis that I defend throughout this short book, namely, that Roman Catholic approaches to the sacrament of confirmation throughout the twentieth century in the United States reflected Catholics' changing self-definition in terms of, or in contrast to, the wider American society. Confirmation, then, serves as a reflection of the relationship between Catholics and the culture.

This thesis has important ramifications for confirmation theology and practice as well as Catholic identity. While theologies of confirmation are anything but uniform throughout the century, there are, nevertheless, some periodic themes that arise. Early in the century, confirmation was widely identified as the sacrament of Catholic Action; it was therefore the sacrament in which Catholics moved from being inward-focused to being outward-focused and were thereby attuned to "see, judge, act" (the motto of Catholic Action) in order to "restore all things in Christ" (the motto of Pope St. Pius X). During the 1960s, while U.S. Catholics saw a large-scale social integration into the wider culture, some theologies of confirmation took on individualistic overtones, even as the dominant theology of the Second Vatican Council rejected the more individualistic bent of neoscholastic sacramental theology. In the next decade, some in the Catholic charismatic renewal adopted confirmation as equivalent to the more Pentecostal "baptism in the Spirit," which, at times, embodied this individualism. In the eighties and following, some theologies of confirmation further developed confirmation as a time for a Catholic's individual choice of his or her religion. More recently, some catechists and theologians lament the results of these theologies and programs of choice, which give rise to such elations as "I memorized everything" or "I got my sacraments," to the detriment of the ongoing relationship between the church and the person. In the past decade or so, voices have arisen that both endorse and decry the many forms, and therefore theologies, that confirmation takes in the church.

While much maligned and hotly debated, the story of confirmation in twentieth-century America also seems to be the story of the ongoing struggle of Catholics to find their identity and place and to create an identity and place for younger Catholics within both American society and the transnational church. I hope that one of the unique contributions of this book is that it foregrounds this struggle in its analysis of confirmation.

As it works across four main periods in the twentieth century, the book takes the form of a theological and catechetical survey of the decades of the twentieth century rather than a strictly narrative history. I attempted to place thinkers, pastors, and teachers in dialogue with one another, so that the reader may observe the general trajectory of the conversation, which I argue is largely influenced by the changing relationship between Catholics and the wider culture. My hope is that the format clearly shows places of overlap between different works as well as making clear references to the works themselves. Insofar as it was practically possible, I have quoted directly from primary sources in order to maintain their integrity and exact language, especially because in many places that language is crucial to understanding the author's approach.

While the cultural influence on theology and pastoral work has been duly noted in many places, the uniqueness of the cultural impact on confirmation is that culture does not seem to have affected the other seven sacraments as drastically. One reason for this seems to be the way the following factors and influences progressively came together in the twentieth century: Pope Pius X's lowering the age of First Eucharist, the Catholic Action movement, advances in psychological and educational theory, Vatican II, the dissolution of the immigrant subculture in America, and the Catholic charismatic movement. Confirmation's particular place in the midst of the transition to adulthood left it susceptible to theological and pastoral adaptation.

Each chapter of the book treats a particular period in the twentieth century. The periodization grew out of the sources and is based upon developments in confirmation conversations, especially as they pertain to specific developments and movements in Catholic life.

While many historians have divided the first half of the twentieth century into smaller periods, for the purposes of studying confirmation,

I have decided to mark 1910 to 1959 as one large period, not because I wish to assert that all theology leading up to the Second Vatican Council was flatline, but rather because the shifts that do occur throughout this period fit, in some sense, under the Catholic Action umbrella, which dominated the consciousness of Catholics in terms of their relationship to the wider transcontinental church and to the wider society. The liturgical renewal, also a driving force in the confirmation conversation, was itself connected to Catholic Action and confirmation in interesting ways. The end of this period coincides with Debra Campbell's end mark for what she calls the "Heyday of Catholic Action."[1]

The 1960s seemed tumultuous enough to merit an entire chapter. William Portier cites the 1960s as the time in which Catholics moved out of Catholic neighborhoods and into the suburbs. By the end of this decade Portier says, Catholics were virtually statistically indistinguishable from other citizens.[2] In addition to this "dissolution of the subculture," this period saw *ressourcement* theology at its apogee, the Second Vatican Council, and the beginnings of the interplay of psychological theory and sacramental theology. All of these had their effects on both confirmation and Catholics' self-definition. These stories, of confirmation and Catholics' self-understanding in the twentieth century, should not be isolated but rather considered in light of one another. Taken together, the events and movements of the sixties serve as a turning point insofar as they set the stage for confirmation's development after 1971.

The Catholic charismatic renewal formally began at Duquesne University in 1967. Its major influence on the theology of confirmation, however, did not bubble up until the following decade around the time of and following the promulgation of the revised rite of confirmation by Pope Paul VI in 1971. Therefore, I consider the charismatic renewal's impact on confirmation in a chapter dedicated to the years between 1971 and 1980. In addition to bearing the marks of the charismatic renewal and the revised rite, confirmation in this decade continued to serve as the canvas upon which the relationship of U.S. Catholics to their wider pluralistic culture was painted. As Catholics continue to become less distinct from their fellow U.S. citizens, confirmation becomes a time for younger Catholics to choose the church from among an increasing number of religious options offered by a pluralistic society.

In the final period after 1981, the charismatic renewal takes a back seat to the confirmation question while confirmation begins to absorb the characteristic individualist emphasis of American culture in a particular manner. What drives this period is a growing sense of individualism among Catholics, noted by many American Catholic historians. In line with the argument made throughout this book, confirmation theology and pastoral reflections seem to match this growing individualism with a strong emphasis on confirmation as the time of individual choice. During this same period, many catechists and pastoral associates begin to recognize, and criticize, young people's exodus from parish life after confirmation, what they come to call "confirmation as graduation." The chapter suggests that these two tendencies—to theologize confirmation as a time of individual choice and to exit parish life following it—are deeply related.

The development of this particular approach to confirmation and its accompanying problems grows to be something of a major subtext of this work. If confirmation theology reflects, in some measure, Catholics' relationship to the wider culture, by the end of the twentieth century that influence has reached a level at which confirmation has unintentionally begun to undercut Catholic identity. The conclusion, then, makes some general suggestions about the direction of the confirmation conversation and points to some particular approaches to confirmation that hold promise for addressing the contemporary context.

Some, especially in the later twentieth century, deem confirmation "the forgotten sacrament." While such a designation proves accurate from one angle, from others confirmation appears to be absolutely central to numerous important Catholic movements in the United States. Scratching the surface a bit, it quickly becomes clear that confirmation received no shortage of attention from theologians and catechists in the United States throughout the twentieth century. Certainly in some cases, this attention betrays the lack of attention given it by Catholics in the pews and serves as a sort of rallying cry for the importance of the sacrament. There are, however, also cases, such as the Catholic charismatic movement, where the excitement over confirmation is much more organic and is even a gesture of revitalizing the recognition of the Spirit's presence in the life of the church at large.

A few words are necessary, then, about the sources that built this project. I have made no attempt to be comprehensive in composing the bibliography, but tried to be reasonably representative of all the major themes and developments of confirmation in the twentieth century. I have included a number of sources generally absent from strictly theological writings about confirmation —pamphlets, letters to editors, educational manuals and textbooks, and articles in catechetical periodicals—in addition to some major theological books and articles. I have also made use of selective historical studies that address the issues pertinent to the development of confirmation in the United States.

I hope that with this unique collection of sources, the book contributes something valuable to the ongoing conversation. I also hope that my work shows the importance of the work that already has been done on confirmation. Many have been tempted to throw up their proverbial arms in theological and pastoral frustration with all that has been written and said about confirmation over the past century. Yet, the theology of confirmation has been at the center of the relationship between Catholics and the wider culture in the United States. This work shows that confirmation, unlike any other sacrament, has served as a cipher for Catholics' place in the wider American context and as a location for working out that identity. This has important implications for the present. We need to discern, as a church, what sort of relationship between Catholics and the wider culture the sacrament of confirmation is instilling in the mostly younger Catholics who receive the sacrament in the twenty-first century. We need, then, to ask important questions about that relationship, which this book only begins to ask. In other words, we need to be more self-reflective about the interplay between the church's place in the culture and sacramental/catechetical practice. In still other words, we should think deeply about the ways that Catholicism has been inculturated in the United States along with the challenges and opportunities unique to the American church, and this reflection must be connected to our sacramental and catechetical practices.

In Louis-Marie Chauvet's discussion of initiation in his magnum opus *Symbol and Sacrament*, he speaks of a series of paradoxes that must remain in an "unstable equilibrium" if Christian initiation is to be able to function well. Among these paradoxes he lists, "the necessity of setting an end to the initiation process, an end which, however, never truly arrives in Christianity."[3] In some ways this study may be seen as an attempt to exhort Catholics to do a better job of "holding up both ends of the chain," to use the words of Henri de Lubac, of this paradox. The development of confirmation in the American context has, largely because of the wider individualism of the culture, too heavily emphasized the former aspect of this initiation paradox such that the latter has largely been obscured. It is the sagging of that latter end of the chain, among other things, that I experienced firsthand and inspired me to write this book.

Chapter 1

Confirmation, the Liturgical Movement, and Catholic Action: 1910–1959

Quam Singulari

> The age of discretion, both for Confession and for Holy Communion, is the time when a child begins to reason, that is about the seventh year, more or less. From that time on begins the obligation of fulfilling the precept of both Confession and Communion.[1]

With these words of August 1910, the Sacred Congregation of the Discipline of the Sacraments under Pope Pius X laid bare the troubled underbelly of confirmation without even mentioning it. The congregation clearly identified the oft-cited and variously interpreted "age of reason or discretion" with the seventh year. Prior to the decree, First Eucharist was not permitted before age twelve and was sometimes received as late as sixteen.[2] Confirmation was normally celebrated around age seven, sometimes as late as twelve, but nearly always before First Communion. As such, it rested between the two more highly regarded sacraments of baptism and First Eucharist and escaped any distinction as the last in the regular order of sacraments received by school-age Catholics. Along with his encyclical *Acerbo Nimis*, which canonically established the Confraternity of Christian Doctrine (CCD) in every parish,[3] this shift in the time of reception of Communion was one of the primary reasons why St. Pius X would later be popularly referred to as "the pope of little children."[4]

1

Initially, however, the decree was not entirely well received in the United States, as those in pastoral roles quickly became concerned about the depth of catechesis children would attain by age seven.[5] Parents, they worried, would have no good reason to continue to bring their children to catechetical classes if the children had already received Communion.

Over the years, concerns over the first reception of Communion transformed into devotion to St. Pius X, who had brought communion to the children,[6] and new pastoral issues would emerge on the horizon. The Holy See's well-intentioned move to indicate the normal age for the reception of First Eucharist had opened the door for delaying confirmation to the teenage years (the years during which young Christians had first approached the Communion rail prior to the decree) as a sort of sacramental carrot on the stick of catechists.

While many scholars describe how delaying confirmation became widespread across the decades following *Quam Singulari*, another reading understands *Quam Singulari* as a response to one particular aspect of the liturgical renewal—the practice of giving Communion to children at a younger age during Mass—that had arisen in nineteenth-century France amid increasing emphasis on the connection between the celebration of the Mass and the eucharistic elements.[7]

The challenges of proper catechesis paired with the theological questions that arose out of confirmation's new position in the order of reception opened up the sacrament to a variety of applications. In the following decades, confirmation would be given a prominent place in two key movements in the early twentieth-century church: Catholic Action and the liturgical movement. Indeed, confirmation was one major point of contact between these two movements.

During this period, in particular, the work of Thomas Aquinas on confirmation served as both a benchmark and a theological paradigm out of which approaches to the sacrament were often developed and discussed. The neo-Thomistic paradigm places certain themes foremost in confirmation theology throughout this period: the strengthening of the confirmand, the more perfect indwelling of the Holy Spirit, transition into ecclesial adulthood, a distinction between active and passive characters, and the relationship between baptism and confirmation. Though it is most explicit in this particular period, the discussion throughout the entire century can be characterized, in one sense, as an ongoing attempt to reconcile these categories with new developments. For example, with the injection of psychological theory into confirmation theology and catechesis in general, new questions are raised about maturity that St. Thomas did not address. Most of those writing about confirmation as it pertains to the liturgical movement and to Catholic Action are working within the neo-Thomistic categories that they have inherited and are applying them to the new socio-political situation.

Loyal church reformers championed the liturgical movement, while Catholic Action became Pius X's and Pius XI's prescription for Catholics' primary mode of engagement with the European political climate. The call for Catholic Action would continue to grow throughout the coming decades. Stateside, the largely immigrant Catholic population existed primarily in Catholic "ghettoes," which were not generally considered part of larger American society, fueling an uneasy, somewhat unique relationship with "the world" in the U.S. church. When, as we will see, confirmation becomes the sacrament of Catholic Action, Catholics in the United States see it particularly through the lens of this social situation. Catholic Action and the liturgical movement were major components of the Catholic revival in America and both had a marked impact on confirmation's early twentieth-century shape.[8]

Confirmation and the Liturgical Movement

In the decades immediately following *Quam Singulari*, Pius X's push for increased reception of the Eucharist spurred lay involvement in the liturgical movement, particularly in Europe.[9] Inspired by the zeal he encountered on a trip to Europe in 1925, Virgil Michel, a Benedictine priest from St. John's Abbey in Collegeville, Minnesota, "launched the journal *Orate Fratres* [later, *Worship*] to popularize

Pope Leo XIII's 1899 condemnation of "Americanism" stifled much American theological creativity and even as that creativity began to take new forms during the period under discussion, fears lingered. For those reasons, theology in the United States leaned heavily on European developments that had themselves been severely chastened in 1907 by Pius X's condemnation of "Modernism" in *Pascendi Dominici Gregis*. St. Thomas was seen as the bedrock theological source for the Catholic tradition largely because of Leo XIII's *Aeterni Patris* (1879), which had become even more important in the post-*Pascendi* context. *Aeterni Patris* designated the Angelic Doctor's thought normative for all Catholic theology and philosophy, hence, the rise and near dominance of Catholic neo-Thomism. *Pascendi Dominici Gregis* (1907) was, along with *Lamentabili Sane Exitu* (1907), one of two curial documents condemning Modernism. There is, of course, much debate about the extent to which neo-Thomist appeals to St. Thomas are indeed accurate articulations and legitimate developments of his thought.

the liturgical movement that he had encountered in Europe the year before, and it soon became a primary catalyst in the American Catholic liturgical movement."[10] Michel also made the theology of the Mystical Body of Christ integral to the vision of *Orate Fratres*, which boasted an unusually high number of lay subscribers.[11] Confirmation occupied the pages of *Orate Fratres* quite soon after its inception. In the years that followed, *Orate Fratres* became a veritable chronicle for the development of reform-minded pastoral and theological thought on confirmation.

In 1928, after fellow Benedictine Basil Stegmann published a piece entitled "Confirmation, the Armor of the Soul," in which he argued that confirmation should be celebrated "soon after the years of infancy" in line with present practice,[12] Michel published a three-part article on confirmation extended over the next three issues of *Orate Fratres*.[13] Michel's work echoes Stegmann's in some ways, but also offers some different emphases. Reflecting on the chrism signed on the confirmand's head, Michel notes that confirmation "is the one time in the life of every faithful that he comes in direct contact with the power of Christ in its Apostolic abundance."[14]

The language of "soldier for Christ" and its corresponding warfare imagery, having deep roots in the tradition, was common throughout this period.[15]

Prima facie Michel's assertion might seem to deny the encounter with Christ in the other sacraments, yet the uniqueness of confirmation is indicated in the final two words—"*Apostolic* abundance." The encounter with the bishop, the successor of the apostles, in confirmation confers apostolic responsibility on the confirmand; it is "the coming of age of the Christian soul."[16] This apostolic responsibility would be a clear link for Michel and others when articulating points of contact between liturgical celebrations and the active Christian mission to the world. It is evident from his work that Michel swims in rising theological currents, pushing increased lay participation in the church and the world. Indeed, Catholic Action was also known as "the lay apostolate."

The phrase "soldiers for Christ" and its attendant imagery of warfare were widespread and official in the tradition during this period. Both Stegmann and Michel heavily rely on such imagery in their theologies. Stegmann uses the imagery in a passive manner and Michel in a more active one. Evident from his subtitle, for Stegmann, the strengthening of confirmation is that of protection or "armor." For Michel, confirmation is an impulse, a spur toward the active Christian life, evident in his third subtitle, "Call to Battle."

The different uses of the imagery are reflected in the *Baltimore Cate-chism*. There is a shift from the more internally focused verbs of the 1885 edition, which stress submission, "We are called soldiers of Jesus Christ to indicate how we must *resist* the attacks of our spiritual enemies and secure our victory over them by *following* and *obeying* Our Lord," to the verbs of the 1949 edition, which stress action, "A confirmed person is called a soldier of Christ because, through confirmation, he is especially deputed to *profess* the faith *strongly* and to *fight* for it."[17] Michel is thus a precursor to the more official revisions that would come with the new, revised edition of the *Baltimore Catechism* (1949) and, before that, the pontificate of Pius XI (1922–39).

Michel places striking weight upon the sacrament of confirmation. Following Aquinas, he elaborates an ontological distinction between baptism and confirmation, endorsing St. Thomas's position that baptism is movement from nonbeing to being and confirmation movement from being to perfect being.[18] "Perfect" here is meant in the traditional sense of "being essentially complete" rather than in its contemporary popular sense. The implications of this ontological distinction are again active ones. Michel argues that baptism initiates the possibility of living supernaturally and perhaps lessens its difficulties, whereas confirmation nearly eradicates these difficulties by the gifts of the Holy Spirit.[19] This assumes, however, cooperation with the supernatural powers received at confirmation. Michel writes, "Now that we have received the grace of Confirmation, *what are we going to do about it? Forget it?* Or remember it as a festive event of our past lives and nothing more?" and further, "The graces of Confirmation will therefore come to full effect only if put to active use in life; and only if thus put to use, will the fruits of the Spirit come into actuality."[20] Without concrete Christian action, these graces of the sacrament are not fully realized.

In the liturgy Michel saw an educative remedy to American individualism and materialism.[21] His theology of confirmation was clearly of a piece with his pursuit of liturgical renewal in the U.S. church as well as his Thomistic theological tones. To this end, Michel encourages parishes to celebrate confirmation as an event for which the *entire parish* prepares extensively and identifies the home as a place of continued encouragement to live out the graces of confirmation.[22]

With his emphasis on the apostolic gift to the laity in confirmation, Michel's articles display the undercurrents of lay involvement in the church that rise to the fore following the Great Depression and are supplemented by the American church's reception of Pius XI's *Quadragesimo Anno* (1931). Debra Campbell writes:

> The depression was [an] important catalyst in the changing self
> perceptions of the Catholic community. It reawakened the social
> consciences of the laity, prompting what Donald Thorman described
> as the rebirth of the lay apostolate, virtually dormant (as a mass
> movement) since the demise of lay congresses in the 1890s. . . .
> This new impulse toward a more strenuous effort to promote social
> justice among the urban poor was reinforced by the appearance of
> the social encyclical *Quadragesimo Anno* in 1931.[23]

This new-found fervor for social action would become more explicit
about a decade later in theologies of confirmation emphasizing the socio-
political implications of the sacrament, beyond the internal, spiritual
ones. Indeed Pius XI's social encyclical was written to combat the "evil
individualist spirit of the age,"[24] a spirit against which Michel and the
liturgical movement in the United States vigorously fought.

In 1931, the same year that *Quadragesimo Anno* was promulgated,
the Pontifical Commission for Authentically Interpreting the Canons of
the Code dashed the hopes of some catechists who wished for a later
confirmation by reaffirming canon 788 of the 1917 Code of Canon Law,
which found age seven most suitable for the celebration of confirmation.[25] The reaffirmation resulted in a pastoral conundrum. For catechists and pastors who strove to uphold both *Quam Singulari* and the
Code of Canon Law, it was improper to confer confirmation after First
Communion, as was a growing trend, and it was impossible to confer
confirmation beforehand, as had been common practice prior to *Quam
Singulari*, because confirmation could not be celebrated before age seven
and the reception of Eucharist was to begin at age seven.[26] It seemed
that the only available option was to celebrate confirmation and First
Eucharist concurrently or at least in the same year, an option seemingly
not widely taken. What was solidified, it seems, was the link between
confirmation and responsibility.

Confirmation understood as Christian responsibility took on a decidedly social cast. H. A. Reinhold, for example, drawing explicitly on
Quadragesimo Anno, argues that the "responsibility" of confirmation requires Christians to invest in a socially conscious manner and "to tackle
this modern scourge of capitalism . . . in the name of the sacramental
life of the Church."[27] In an epigram to the article, Reinhold cites the
cardinals of Milan and Malines who write that Catholic Action must be
liturgical or will cease to exist; Reinhold himself connects sacramental
worship to social responsibility via confirmation. Thus, confirmation

works as the buttress for this all-important link between lay social action and the liturgy.

Confirmation and Catholic Action

The social encyclicals, the misery of the Great Depression, and the uneasiness of the interbellum period gave added urgency and vigor to the Catholic Action movement. Historian Debra Campbell defines Catholic Action: "From the '30s through the '50s, the terms 'Catholic Action' and 'lay apostolate' were extensively used by Catholic bishops, priests, and lay people to refer to the laity's recently rediscovered responsibility to take action on the Church's behalf."[28] Increased lay involvement in the life of the church, both internally and externally, was encouraged since the beginning of the twentieth century and continued to grow throughout the next fifty years under the designation "Catholic Action."

Five years prior to *Quam Singulari*, Pius X had described the goal of Catholic Action in his encyclical *Il Fermo Proposito*—"the restoration of all things in Christ." Campbell explains, "Pius X declared that he needed 'the cooperation' of both the clergy and the faithful in fulfilling his pastoral office. He added that 'in truth, we are called . . . to build up that unique body of which Christ is the Head, a body which is highly organized . . . and well coordinated in all its movements.' "[29] Pius X's encyclical, paired with the mandate that every parish implement a CCD program in the same year (1905), furthered Leo XIII's overtures toward lay activism and set the stage for "the Catholic Action pope" Pius XI. Theodore Hesburgh discusses Pius XI's emphasis on Catholic Action:

> From his first encyclical letter, *Ubi Arcano* [1922], which sounded a general call to the lay apostolate, to his last encyclical, *Con Singular Complacentia* [1939], published on the day of his death, exhorting the hierarchy of the Philippines to strengthen their organization of Catholic Action, his writings and addresses are ever insistent on this one point [Catholic Action] . . . he takes care to remark many times over that this apostolate of the laity is not an innovation but a *re-emphasis of what is traditional in the Church*.[30]

In 1934, Pius XI referred to baptism and confirmation as the sacraments of Catholic Action—baptism insofar as it makes one a member of the Mystical Body of Christ and confirmation in a more obvious way, making confirmandi *"Iesu Christi milites"*: soldiers for Jesus Christ.[31] In so doing, Pius fomented connections between the active work of the laity and the apostolic character of confirmation. The link between Catholic Action and confirmation became more explicit and more widespread.

In 1941, *Orate Fratres* reprinted an article from *New Blackfriars* by English Dominican Gerard Meath.[32] Meath's article explores the connection between confirmation and the lay apostolate:

> The nature and the degree of . . . sharing in the Priesthood of Christ varies considerably in the different grades within the Church; but it is a reality even in the lowest grade and gives an almost unbelievable quality and value to even the most commonplace participation in the liturgical life of the Church; and the source of this sacerdotal power throughout all the hierarchical grades is to be found in the Sacraments. Moreover, as far as Catholic Action in the modern sense is concerned, there is a particularly important source to be recognized in the Sacrament of Confirmation.[33]

Meath associates "layman's Holy Orders" with public witness, full membership in the church, and spiritual maturity.[34] The seed that had been planted by Michel was bearing fruit in the form of confirmation's association with Catholic Action.

Benedictine Damasus Winzen, without calling confirmation the sacrament of Catholic Action, discusses the apostolic mission of the laity inaugurated at confirmation. He writes, "Knowing the catechism is no more than knowing the ABC's. You must become a teacher, a missionary, an 'apostle'! As a confirmed Christian you have an official mission and therefore also a definite responsibility towards the 'hundred millions' in our country who do not know Christ and towards the many more millions all over the world who are ignorant of God."[35] Winzen's understanding of the lay apostolate is shaped by the post World War II context; he laments that even though Catholics outnumber Communists in the United Nations, there is no mention of God in its proceedings.[36]

Like St. Thomas, Winzen draws a clear distinction between baptism and confirmation, describing the years after baptism as the beginning stage of the Christian life during which Catholics remain self-focused, but the character of confirmation, he argues, "transcends the narrow circle of personal salvation and authorizes to actions that have reference to the Church as a whole."[37] Displaying some of the period's contentiousness of Catholics in the United States with the Protestant majority, Winzen blames Protestants' rejection of sacramental confirmation for their "[inability] to develop a really Christian civilization," since "confirmation is the sacrament of the *plenitude* of Christ."[38] This plenitude, Winzen asserts, can be found in the symbolism of chrism, for "the material which is used in confirmation . . . is a mixture of olive oil and balm. The mixture itself indicates the inner wealth of the Spirit who, being one, is manifold in His works."[39] Winzen continues by discussing the gifts of the Holy Spirit, the Spirit's indwelling in the Christian person, and the fragrance of the chrism which, emanating from the confirmandi, fills the entire church like the Holy Spirit. The chrism, consecrated by the bishop, also symbolizes the confirmandi's apostolic mission as they are "made co-workers of the clergy in a special way."[40]

Writing in 1947, the same year that Pius XII greatly encouraged the liturgical movement via his encyclical *Mediator Dei*, Dominican James R. Gillis notes a shift toward ecclesial responsibility in the way that confirmandi see themselves, "Today the confirmed are less inclined to see their consecration merely in the terms of their own private matter against the world, the flesh, and the devil, and are more inclined to recognize their responsibility to the Church."[42] Gillis is at pains to broaden the emphasis on the internal "battle of the soul" that confirmation helps to fight. The individual's interior life in the Spirit, Gillis argues, is not merely a precursor for Catholic Action, but constitutive of it. In conjunction with making adults out of "spiritual children," confirmation is, for Gillis, the sacrament of the lay apostolate.[43] He writes, "the real case for confirmation will be written by a living apostolate made fresh by the breath of the Holy Ghost" and, in turn, "Catholics will not heed this call [to take their place in the apostolic mission of the church] until they begin to find it necessary to call upon that strengthening grace of confirmation frequently and fervently."[44]

Deeper reflections on the Mystical Body of Christ theology, tied to the liturgical movement and to Pius XII's encyclical *Mystici Corporis* (1943), prompted some to reconceive the sacraments as "the vital functions of

In 1946, Anglican Benedictine Gregory Dix published a groundbreaking study based on patristic texts, in which he argued that confirmation is of superior importance to baptism in that baptism has a negative effect (cleansing from sin) and confirmation a positive one (the grace of the Holy Spirit). Dix's work precipitated new conversation on the relationship between the two among Anglicans and non-Anglicans alike, conversation which would endure throughout the following decades. For Catholics, the significant questions coming out of this debate concerned the character of confirmation in relation to that of baptism and how to understand the workings of the Holy Spirit in each of the sacraments.[41]

that Body."[45] George Smith's article in 1952 is indicative of this move. Like those considered previously, Smith continues to stress the distinction between baptism and confirmation in terms of childhood and adulthood. He emphasizes, quoting St. Thomas, that children are naturally individualistic; therefore, baptism helps them in the realm of individual spiritual growth. The responsibility to bear witness, to reach outside of oneself, comes with "spiritual maturity" in the church, brought about by confirmation.[46] Bearing witness further corresponds to one's place "in the organism of the Mystical Body."[47] The Spirit, Smith argues, guides the church, but in confirmation comes upon the individual Christian to make witness possible over and against the world, whose spirit is inimical to the church.[48]

While Smith's emphasis on witness according to one's role in the Mystical Body of Christ is novel, his understanding of the active and social implications of confirmation are in line with the growing emphasis of the previous few decades.

The tensile relationship between the church in the United States and the wider culture will prove deeply influential in the theologies that will develop throughout the remainder of the twentieth century. The traditional distinction between the inimical "world" and the Christian life takes on a specific tone and a tangible reality among the predominately immigrant Catholic population struggling to be legitimate citizens of the United States. Confirmation, as with Smith and many who follow, becomes emblematic of the Catholic attempt to negotiate the gap between Catholic culture and "the world." The boundaries of "the world" and Catholics' posture toward it are in no way univocal and neither is confirmation theology.

To sum up, from 1910 to 1959, theologians and pastors associated confirmation with both Catholic Action and the liturgical movement in the United States—both movements that dealt with the relationship between Catholics and "the world." Both movements strove to awaken the laity to their role in evangelizing the world through witness, and social and political action. As such, confirmation has found a place, following *Quam Singulari*, as the sacrament of Christian responsibility. For American Catholic movers and shakers, Catholics became active and attentive to the tensions between their church and their culture following their reception of confirmation.

Chapter 2

Confirmation and the Second Vatican Council: 1960–1971

If the first half of the twentieth century had been characterized by movements aimed at awakening the laity to their role in the church and the world, the period from 1960 to 1971 was characterized by a reconfiguration of the way in which the very terms "church" and "world" functioned in American Catholic discourse. No longer was it so clear that "the world" stood entirely outside of the Catholic subculture in which many U.S. Catholics had been formed. As the first generations of Catholics began to be raised beyond this subculture, "the world" now penetrated every aspect of Catholic life. Catholic formation changed from a mode in which Catholics lived and breathed Catholic culture to one in which Catholics lived and breathed American cultural and religious pluralism. While Catholic Action and the liturgical movement had made strides in rallying the Catholic laity, though not always in the way the popes and bishops had imagined, the terms according to which they operated were not directly transferable to the new socio-political situation of Catholics in the United States.[1] Theological developments, too, disqualified the Catholic Action ecclesiological framework that had made too

An example of the tension between the liturgical movement and the bishops may be found in the Grail Movement, a women's movement that had connections to both Catholic Action and liturgical renewal. This organization upset Archbishop Samuel Stritch of Chicago in 1942 by their failure to emphasize that the laity take their cues from the bishops.

firm distinctions both between the laity and the clergy and between the church and the world. The fragmentation of American culture—in the form of separations between political action, charity work, worship, private prayer, and so on—began to undercut the hope of the liturgical movement to unite liturgy and social action.

Combined with developments in sacramental theology and the work of the Second Vatican Council, the dissolution of the subculture had marked effects on confirmation. As Catholic Action lost steam and the liturgical movement reached a new stage in the work of the Second Vatican Council, it became necessary for confirmation to find a new theological and pastoral home. This chapter will demonstrate how confirmation shifted from its place as the sacrament of Catholic Action and of the liturgical movement to the sacrament in which a Catholic proclaims Catholicism as her religion of choice. The latter theology appears in some texts at the very end of this period, but will reach its height a decade later, after other approaches come forward in the later '70s. The major shift in confirmation theology and practice that occurred during this period is due to at least four factors, which will be considered in turn: (1) the theological paradigm shift leading up to the Second Vatican Council; (2) the promulgation and reception of Vatican II's Constitution on Sacred Liturgy; (3) the "dissolution of the Catholic subculture" in the United States; and (4) the assimilation of psycho-social anthropological theory into catechetical and theological thought.

A "New" Theology

Leo XIII's encyclical *Aeterni Patris* (1879) cemented neoscholasticism as *the* Catholic theology, a very rare phenomenon in the history of a church that has always had a plurality of theological sensibilities and methods (for example, Pauline/Johannine; Alexandrian/Antiochene; Dominican/Franciscan/Ignatian). Dissatisfied with the methods and results of neoscholastic theology, some mid-twentieth century Dominicans and Jesuits began to rediscover the myriad riches of the church's theological heritage and to bring those riches to bear upon contemporary questions. *Nouvelle théologie*, as it was known by its detractors, was a somewhat heterogeneous movement guided by the principle that theology should be done in service to the church's engagement with the contemporary milieu via a *ressourcement*, or a creative "return to the sources."[2] These sources begin with Scripture and extend across the tradition, with a particular focus on patristic texts. As part of their *ressourcement*, these theologians also undertook a careful re-reading of St. Thomas's writings that had been filtered through various modern Thomistic commentators throughout the neoscholastic period.

Edward Schillebeeckx, though not part of the *nouvelle théologie* movement precisely defined, received his doctorate from Le Saulchoir in Etoilles, France, the Dominican bastion of *nouvelle théologie*. Schillebeeckx caught the attention of many by his methodological fusion of Thomistic theology and phenomenology. One of the first fruits of Schillebeeckx's work was in the area of sacramental theology. Joseph Martos explains, "Schillebeeckx was instrumental in showing that Catholicism could develop a theology of the sacraments which was both faithful to the insights of Thomas Aquinas and free of the minimalistic tendency of late scholasticism. Like Aquinas he attempted to recapture the religious experience within the sacramental ritual and then to speak about the experience in philosophical terms, but the basic terms he chose came not from Aristotelian philosophy but from contemporary existentialism."[3] Along with Karl Rahner and Henri de Lubac, Schillebeeckx ushered in the well-known revolution in sacramental theology which, reacting against neoscholastic approaches, marks the sacraments as "milestones" in a broader Christian sacramental way of life.[4] He identifies Christ as the primordial sacrament of God and the church as the sacrament of Christ, connecting the sacraments to Christ via the church in a real, but less mechanical way than had been conceived. Schillebeeckx uses the phenomenological term "encounter" to describe the sacraments; through these encounters, the faithful enter more deeply into the mystery of Christ, and in turn, grow in their relationship with God.[5] In light of Schillebeeckx's work in the late fifties and early sixties, sacramental theology generally became less focused on the specific graces and characters of the sacrament and more oriented toward the formative character of these "encounters."[6]

The *nouvelle théologie* movement burgeoned mainly at two French houses of study: the Dominican seminary, Le Saulchoir, and the Jesuit house of study, Fourvière, just outside of Lyon. The former included such notable theologians as Marie-Dominique Chenu and Yves Congar on the faculty; the latter employed Henri de Lubac, Jean Daniélou, Hans Urs von Balthasar, and Henri Bouillard.

This renewal of the historical depth of theological work seriously challenged the close association between Catholic Action and confirmation. In the United States, Ursuline sister Marian Bohen offers an example of the influence of *ressourcement* theology on confirmation. Identifying the wide range of confirmation theologies at play, including those of important contemporary European theologians such as Louis Bouyer, Charles Journet, Rahner, and Schillebeeckx, Bohen began her in-depth study of confirmation with the conviction that confirmation is best understood as the sacrament of Catholic Action, an association that we saw develop during the previous decades, but also extended into this period particularly in catechetical pastoral pamphlets.[7] After serious historical study, Bohen abandoned this position in favor of understanding confirmation as the *mystērion* of the Holy Spirit. The narrow association of this age-old sacrament with the modern Catholic Action movement seemed to betray its theological richness. Instead, Bohen draws upon the Greek root, *mystērion*, from which "sacrament" is ultimately derived, in order to highlight the revelation of "mystery" in the sacrament, a sense which Bohen argues had been lost in identifying confirmation primarily as the sacrament of Catholic Action.[8] Drawing on Schillebeeckx's theology of the church as the sacrament of Christ, Pius XII's *Mystici Corporis*, and numerous New Testament texts, Bohen asserts that "Christ and the Church are one by quasi-identity," leading her to conclude that the sacraments are mysterious (in the sense of *mystērion*) encounters with Christ's passion, death, and resurrection.[9] Of confirmation she writes,

> The reality which is called the Holy Spirit is Charity, and so it is he who pours forth this reality, this power from on high, this "Godliness" into Christian hearts. To this reality does the Spirit bear witness before the world as he purifies, enlightens, strengthens, and perfects the children of God. In reflecting and radiating this reality, confirmed Christians are *mystēria* of the Church in Christ. . . . The sacrament of confirmation is the *mystērion* of the Holy Spirit. This sacrament is, then, the revelation in symbol of that power of God in man which is most radically opposed to "world" and "flesh."[10]

Bohen recovers the understanding of the Holy Spirit as love from the annals of patristic and scholastic trinitarian theology to describe confirmation as the "seal of Love." She finds this theology able to address problems that cannot be addressed by Catholic Action theology, such as why the church confirms in danger of death. She also argues, based on her theology of the Holy Spirit, that the anointing of confirmation deepens that of baptism in degree, but not in kind.[11]

Bohen's investigation of the fathers also led her to re-emphasize confirmation as a "sacrament of initiation" and, therefore, its connection to baptism and Eucharist; she writes, "According to the earliest liturgies and patristic testimony, baptism-confirmation-Eucharist formed one 'rite' of Christian initiation, and it is only in this framework that the signifying mysteries of baptism and confirmation can be understood."[12] She describes confirmation as the second stage of initiation, in which the Holy Spirit completes the Christian's death and rebirth in Christ begun in baptism. Eucharist is the third and culminating stage of Christian initiation. Bohen draws out the catechetical implications of her revised theology, arguing that "reasoning power is not an essential requisite for confirmation. Therefore, the argument that the soldier of Christ must know the faith he is defending and thus should not be confirmed unless he shows sufficient knowledge of the content of the catechism is not a valid one."[13] She further distills the catechetical implications of her position a year later in an article in *Worship*: "Confirmation is of a piece with baptism and the Eucharist, so that to separate it from these two sacraments is to lose something vital to its meaning. . . . The catechesis of confirmation, therefore, should necessarily follow on baptism and precede the child's first reception of the bread of the Eucharist. . . . Catechetical preparation on confirmation itself should naturally center on the person of the Holy Spirit, and the best way of communicating some realization of the reality of his personality would be through the use of biblical and liturgical images."[14]

Bohen's work elicits three conclusions indicative of the theological shift in the first half of the decade. First, influenced by the "return to the sources," Bohen groups baptism, confirmation, and Eucharist together as "sacraments of initiation," terminology which became official at the Second Vatican Council. Second, and connected to the first, she argues that the "soldier for Christ" theology tied to Catholic Action and prominent throughout the first half of the twentieth century cannot hold water in light of early church practice and patristic theology.[15] Third, she mines some of confirmation's theological richness from patristic and scholastic theologies of the Holy Spirit, associating confirmation with the "seal of Love" and the mutual Love between the Father and the Son. This *ressourcement* will shape the questions surrounding confirmation across the next few decades.

In the Wake of *Sacrosanctum Concilium*

Promulgated in 1963, the same year that Bohen's book was published, the Dogmatic Constitution on the Sacred Liturgy, *Sacrosanctum Concilium*, lent official support to the designation "sacraments of initiation" for baptism, confirmation, and Eucharist. The council fathers called for revision to the confirmation rite "so that the intimate connection of this sacrament with the whole of the Christian initiation may more clearly appear."[16] The nature of this "intimate connection" among the sacraments of initiation and how it is best illustrated would become a key question in sacramental theology following the council.

Sacrosanctum Concilium also called for the restoration of the catechumenate,[17] a process of preparation for initiation widely employed in the early church in which those preparing to enter the church are mentored in distinct steps of prayer and catechesis as they move toward readiness for initiation. This early church practice informed the promulgation of the Rite of Christian Initiation for Adults (RCIA) (1972), which established an ordinary ritual in which adults receive all three sacraments of initiation on a single occasion. In the years following its promulgation, many point to the RCIA as the norm for Christian initiation and, therefore, a model for all other celebrations of the sacraments of initiation. *That* the RCIA was to serve as a model for initiation in the church was not generally disputed, but *how* that is to be understood garnered much discussion. Some pointed to the celebration of all three sacraments on one occasion as the norm, some pointed to adult initiation as the norm, and some pointed to the order, baptism-confirmation-Eucharist, as the norm established by the RCIA.[18] These different emphases would prove to be central in the confirmation discussion over the decades to follow.

Sacrosanctum Concilium did not quell the debates about confirmation but it did reconfigure the terms of the discussion. The council fathers did not mention Catholic Action with regard to confirmation, notably not reiterating Pius XI's direct correlation of the two in 1934. They simply called for the clearer expression of unity between baptism and confirmation. The precise nature of this unity became a central theological question in the council's wake, especially after many years had been spent contrasting baptism and confirmation in order to distinguish the manner of grace received in each.[19]

As if she were immediately responding to the concerns of the council, Benedictine professor of religious education Mary Charles Bryce writes about the "isolation" of confirmation both from Christ's saving action in the world and from the other sacraments as the cause of Catholics' inadequate theological treatment of confirmation.[20] More specifically, she perceives confirmation's isolation from the other two sacraments of initiation as problematic. Bryce writes,

There is a hierarchy of sacraments with baptism and eucharist in positions of pre-eminence. While all sacraments must be studied in relation to these two, confirmation has a special affinity to them. Together with baptism and the eucharist it forms a triad—"the sacraments of initiation," as they are called today. *The lack of emphasis on this relational role contributed perhaps more than any other factor to the confusion regarding the function and purpose of the sacrament.* Until more light is thrown on this issue, tangential inquiries or peripheral searchings for the distinctive grace effect of this sacrament will continue.[21]

Bryce finds in *Sacrosanctum Concilium* discouragement of "the longstanding practice . . . at least in this country, of administering the rite [of confirmation] outside a eucharistic celebration," a practice, along with the propensity to delay confirmation for "too long a time after Baptism," which is indicative of sacramental "isolation."[22]

Despite the tension and widespread disagreement brought about by considering confirmation in isolation, Bryce finds three "constants" "appearing early in historical investigation and enjoying an unbroken tradition down to the present" in confirmation theology and practice: (1) confirmation is the completion and perfection of baptismal initiation; (2) in confirmation, the Holy Spirit is bestowed in a special manner; and (3) confirmation effects what the Holy Spirit does.[23] Citing Schillebeeckx and Hans Urs von Balthasar, Bryce offers the redemptive mystery of Christ as a corrective to the confusion over confirmation; she associates baptism with Easter (death to life) and confirmation with Pentecost (the descent of the Holy Spirit). In this way, the two sacraments constitute one mystery, intertwined with God's work of redemption.[24] This move leaves her with the question of the Holy Spirit's work at Pentecost.

Working out of the third "constant" —that confirmation effects what the Holy Spirit does—Bryce pursues confirmation via the Holy Spirit's action. She writes, "The work of the Spirit is to effect the divinization of man."[25] For Bryce, divinization happens primarily on the individual level, albeit in the context of the church. While she mentions the Spirit's (and therefore love's presence) in the church as a whole, Bryce's considerations focus on the Spirit's indwelling in the individual Christian. Of divinization she writes, "A gift freely given, love elicits, hopes for a free response. Unregenerate man is incapable of response in the fullest Christian sense. But one filled with the Spirit is capable. Freedom then, a certain liberation of the person, is likewise a fruit of the Holy Spirit's presence in the community and in the individuals in that community. The

Holy Spirit informs and enflames man bringing him to a true discovery and realization of himself."[26] Here, Bryce mentions the Spirit's dwelling in the community and the individual, but she explains divinization primarily as individual—"liberation of the person," "a true discovery and realization of himself." Confirmation serves as the locus for this personal interrogation and introspection. Bryce's theology purposely avoids "isolating" confirmation from baptism and Eucharist; it does, however place a strong emphasis on the individual confirmand. Since Bryce describes the Spirit's primary dwelling place as one's heart, the psychological development of the person becomes the natural place to turn to understand the grace of confirmation.

Bryce's emphasis on the individual receiving confirmation marks an incipient shift in confirmation theology in which the sacrament serves the development of individual maturity. This new direction differs from the focus on the grace received in the soul of the confirmand by those elaborating a Catholic Action theology in that the former takes maturity as such as a starting point. More will be said about this shift, which involves the role of the social sciences in confirmation theology, in the final section of this chapter. Because, however, the application of these disciplines to theology was largely enabled by Catholics' emergence from the subculture, we turn now to that shift.

Dissolution of the Catholic Subculture

As the sixties rolled on, many Catholics in the United States continually underwent a large-scale entrée into the wider culture out of immigrant Catholic "ghettoes" where, from a young age, the church seemed almost unavoidable. William L. Portier describes this shift as the "dissolution of the subculture,"

> Between World War I and the time of the Second Vatican Council, immigrant Catholics voluntarily built an elaborate subculture centered in the urban Northeast but extending to the cities of the Midwest with outposts as far-flung as Butte, Montana and Shawnee, Oklahoma. A network of parishes, schools at every level, hospitals and other agencies served as a buffer between most Catholics and American religious pluralism. Though geographically diverse, the subculture had a distinctive spiritual and intellectual topography. Not all Catholics went to Catholic schools. But whether they lived

in New Jersey or Oklahoma, they participated in varying degrees in a shared religious culture. They learned similar practices of praying and thinking that added to their demographic distinctiveness. This Catholic world was surely not airtight. But it helped to protect generations of immigrants from Nativism and anti-Catholicism even as it schooled them in how to be Americans. *As a result, most American Catholics never felt the full effects of their country's voluntary religious culture.* As the twentieth century advanced, American Catholics continued to move up the sociological escalator. But as they did, many experienced the subculture as more of a confine than a haven. By mid-century, Catholic elites could refer to their cultural habitat as a "ghetto." Many suffered a loss of confidence. Life seemed more real beyond the "ghetto's" borders. By the 1960s, significant numbers of Catholics had moved to the suburbs. At the end of that decade, demographic differences between Catholics and other Americans became statistically negligible. This dissolution of the subculture is the single most important fact in U. S. Catholic history in the second half of the twentieth century.[27]

The "dissolution of the subculture" played its role, too, in the reorientation of confirmation theology in the United States. Especially throughout the later sixties, some theologians began to describe prevailing confirmation theology as obsolete, particularly in view of the needs of Catholic youth, who now inhabited full-blown pluralism.

One such theologian was Francis Buckley. Unlike some respondents to *Sacrosanctum Concilium*, Buckley did not think that confirmation should be celebrated closer to infant baptism. Instead, he argues that confirmation "should be given when [those who have been baptized as infants] have sufficient psychological and spiritual maturity. For most Catholics this will occur around the time they leave school and enter the world of business and labor. Some few may mature earlier, *just as some Baptists ask for baptism at the age of ten or twelve.* Our fellow Christians have much to tell us on this point, if only we will listen. Let the reception of Confirmation come not at some fixed age but when the recipient feels ready and asks for it."[29] He cites *Sacrosanctum Concilium*'s exhortation to celebrate the liturgy with full,

> I accept Joseph Ratzinger's definition of **pluralism**, which he offers after noting that the initial intent of the term was (as used in turn-of-the-century England) to limit the state's control over its citizens: "Pluralism means that each individual belongs to a plurality of social groupings and that this plurality gives rise to a multiplicity of social roles, none of which can absorb man entirely."[28]

conscious, and active participation, a participation which, he argues, is impossible for the infant.[30] Buckley clearly wrestles with the changing social situation of Catholics in America, even comparing confirmation to baptism as celebrated in the Baptist tradition—a comparison that could not have been taken seriously by Catholics in previous decades, whose identity was constructed by its contradistinction to the Protestant majority.

According to Buckley, official, liturgical, and catechetical arguments for celebrating confirmation around age seven or before are outmoded because they "run counter to recent emphases in sacramental theology and to the findings of sociology and psychology." Canon 788 of the 1917 Code of Canon Law, which marked age seven as the norm for the celebration of confirmation, was written for "a Catholic, not pluralist, society, especially not for a modern, industrial, urbanized, highly mobile society, in which a set of values must be interiorized in each person."[31] The new place of Catholics sounds the death knell for what he regards as an antimodern posture taken by the church throughout the first half of the twentieth century and for the confirmation of that theology to which it gave rise. Confirmation modeled on Baptist baptismal practices, argues Buckley, is much more suitable to the new context.

Whether Buckley's arguments are shaped more fundamentally by the "dissolution of the subculture" or by the broader shift in church-world relations ushered in by Vatican II is debatable. To separate the two might very well be impossible for American Catholics. "The dissolution of the subculture," Portier argues, "is the context in which the Second Vatican Council, and its understanding of the church-world relation in modernity, was received in the United States."[32] In any case, two key currents run through Buckley's approach. First, it promises to reckon with the large-scale integration of Catholics into pluralism (or at least dismisses previous positions for not doing so). Confirmation celebrated around the age of seven, he argues, is not suitable for a pluralistic culture in which young people are confronted with myriad religious traditions and options and are, therefore, in need of a later ritual to solidify their place in the Catholic Church. Second, Buckley makes many claims based on psychological development. Confirmation should be celebrated, he argues, at the time when a young person needs it, psychologically speaking. Such promises and warrants were exceedingly rare, if not completely absent, prior to this period.

Buckley was certainly not alone in making explicit reference to Catholics' new social situation in articulating a theology of confirmation.

Catholics are feeling the upheaval. In fact, there is a common concern for the *interiorization* of values that had been, even rather recently, culturally imbibed. For example, Joseph T. Nolan argues that confirmation should be reconstructed as the sacrament of commitment instead of a sacrament of initiation, since Catholics now grow up in pluralism. A few short years after *Sacrosanctum Concilium* emphasized the congruence of baptism, confirmation, and Eucharist as the three sacraments of initiation, Nolan already finds the mantle of "initiation" lacking for confirmation in the U.S. context. He writes,

> One can use a whole complex of infant and childhood rites if they take place in a supportive community, as part of an integrated, widely accepted value system (ghetto, clan, village, small community, ethic group, or medieval church). Such a community is able to interpret these signs (sacraments) and to be a source of the spirit and truth that will nourish the recipient as he grows into the reality they signify. Also, in a more vertical society, where bishops are lords, priests are fathers, and learning and power are highly concentrated, people do not grow into religious adulthood. But we do not live in this kind of stability, monopoly, or uni-culture. *In a pluralist society one has to make a choice among the lifestyles and value systems that are presented.* A serious choice of the Christian life, or the ideal of witness or service, or the direction of the gospels, could be a powerful expression for a young adult who is making the other vocational choices that will provide the framework of her future. We have no specific form for adult commitment to our faith. . . . Nor do we have any rite for choosing a parish community to which we then commit ourselves as builders of the local church.[33]

Nolan's approach is aimed at what Portier calls America's "voluntary religious culture" in which there are many options and those who maintain their Catholicism will have to do so via the "normal processes of human choice." En route to arguing his position, Nolan does not allow the form of his argument to belie the matter; he tries to find the commonalities between confirmation and other "rituals of commitment" such as the Buddhist "going out" ceremony, an approach not found in earlier theologies. What operates on one level as ecumenical openness, interreligious dialogue, and engagement with the world, operates on another level as an embrace of the individualism associated with modern culture.

At the Intersection of Church and Social Science

Also evident from Buckley's and Nolan's positions is an engagement with contemporary psychological theory.[34] As Catholic ghettoes dissolved into the American melting pot and open antipapism softened, American Catholics became more conversant with burgeoning psycho-social anthropology. In conjunction with a general postconciliar posture of openness to the thinking of "the world," psychological advances were openly harvested for use in catechetics and sacramental theology in ways which they had not been before. These changes resulted in a push for wider education among catechists and ministers of all stripes (many of whom were increasingly lay persons).[35]

Increasing individualism was one by-product of this sea change in Catholic ministry.[36] The anthropological focus on the "ego," American rugged individualist culture, and the empowerment of the individual via educational growth develops quickly into a mutually informing threesome that spirals through ministry beginning in the late sixties.

The dissolution of the subculture increases the place of psychological theory in education, where individual minds are said to be liberated from the stifling mentality of the "ghetto" and religious voluntarism gains some sway.[37] Confirmation was not exempt from the effects of this revolution.

Voluntarism has different meanings in the fields of sociology, philosophy, and theology. In this book "religious voluntarism" and "ecclesiological voluntarism" designates the peculiarly American religious culture of *voluntarily* joining a church in the same way that one might join a scout troop or community organization.

Those who appropriated advances in the field of psychology into confirmation theology did so in two distinguishable ways. Some took the psychological model to be the primary lens through which human development should be seen and then gave confirmation a role in this development. Others took the Christian tradition as first-order, then employed psychological insights to help understand the context of ecclesial development. Both give way to a type of individualism in confirmation, albeit in different degrees.

Returning to Mary Charles Bryce's theology of confirmation provides an example of the former approach. One of the constants that Bryce found among widely varying theologies of confirmation in the sixties was that "confirmation does what the Holy Spirit does." We saw Bryce's discussion of the Holy Spirit's work in divinization. Since she understands the Holy Spirit's work of divinization primarily as an inner grace, psychological anthropology is a natural turn for Bryce. For, to understand the human person is, then, to understand something about the Spirit's work and, in turn, confirmation. When Bryce describes the Holy Spirit's work, she does so in terms of Scripture (quoting John, Acts, and various Pauline epistles). Her anthropological starting point, however, is decidedly general (not Christian-specific) and separate from her theology of the Spirit. She writes,

> From the discovery of man in his alienation, estrangement from God, from himself, and from others (a point at which theology has arrived from another direction), psychology has assisted theology in realizing that man's being is a totalness . . . he attains knowledge and conviction not only through rational judgments and choices, through conscious verbalizations, but through involvement of his total self. Further than this, however, science admits to the deeper mystery of man. "Religion lies at the core and center and substance of the developing ego itself." It is at this depth that man comes to recognize his relation to God.[38]

In Bryce's work, one sees the beginnings of the psychological shift in considerations of the human person (the same shift in which "anthropology" becomes a theological category or even a subdiscipline). She considers the human person in psychological terms and not primarily in theological terms.[39] Out of this anthropological frame, in which she presumably sees the Christian doctrine of original sin, Bryce argues that it is only God who can draw a person out of this alienation. Hence, confirmation plays its role in this de-alienating process, inviting "the Spirit to lavish his gifts and fruits with divine abandon"[40] so that the confirmed might transcend natural human alienation.

Despite Bryce's psychological starting point, her theology of confirmation remains intricately intertwined with the Holy Spirit and the Spirit's gifts. She understands Christian maturity and human beings' free response in terms of the Spirit's continuing work. She writes, "In his Spirit God himself is engaged in bringing human creation to maturity."[41] Invoking Paul, she argues that Christian maturity is something that continually develops in the Spirit. With regard to the free response of the Christian person, she writes, "the Spirit will move, inspire, 'persuade' but he will not coerce. . . . But on the other hand, [man] cannot attain the fullness of Christianity without Jesus' Spirit."[42] Bryce contextualizes human free choice and commitment in the work of the Holy Spirit: "The

Christian's life is not *just* a once-and-for-all automatic 'yes' but a process of commitments which the Spirit assists us in making."[43]

Raymond Collins provides an example of marrying confirmation theology and psycho-social theory, using the latter to understand ecclesial development. Collins makes a distinction between psychological maturity and ecclesial maturity in which the psychological is a prerequisite for the ecclesial. Collins writes, "It is only the Christian who has reached a certain stage of psycho-social development who can be an active and effective sign of the Church's prophetic and redemptive mission."[44] Collins argues that bearing ecclesial witness requires personal maturity and that confirmation is the sacrament of ecclesial maturity. The emphasis is on the individual who develops, and then finds a place bearing the mission of the church. Thus, "Normally it should be conferred only upon those who are able to respond to the grace signified by the sacrament, those who are effectively able to participate in the prophetic and redemptive mission of the Church."[45]

Collins is aware that his theology excludes Catholics who have mental disabilities or are otherwise unable to attain maturity in the psycho-social sense. He is, therefore, forced to consign them to "extraordinary circumstances" which "call for an extraordinary conferral of the sacrament. Thus confirmation can properly be conferred upon the retarded. . . . Likewise, confirmation is to be conferred even upon dying infants. In this case, the sacrament takes on the character of the end or completion of their baptismal initiation into the Church."[46] Collins waives the prerequisite psychological maturity in the case of the dying and those with severe disabilities. In so doing, he reconciles the ecclesial practice of confirming "the least among us" with his theology, though such occasions remain exceptions to his theology rather than integral to it.

Catholics in the United States faced new challenges in their sociological stratum and their interaction with wider U.S. culture in the sixties. Confirmation was appropriated accordingly. Confirmation's place as the "sacrament of Catholic Action," was no doubt weakened by fading papal support for Catholic Action itself. This chapter has, nevertheless, illustrated how the advent and development of *ressourcement* theology leading up to Vatican II poked numerous theological holes in the narrow identification of confirmation with Catholic Action, preferring instead a broader emphasis on the role of the Holy Spirit and the interconnection of baptism and confirmation. *Sacrosanctum Concilium* endorsed the connection between baptism, confirmation, and Eucharist, calling them "the sacraments of initiation." In the United States, the dissolution of the immigrant Catholic subculture served as the context for receiving Vatican II's reforms. Paired with a general theological revitalization, this major shift in the way that American Catholics interact with the larger culture prompted some to decry previous theologies on the grounds that they do not fit the current worldly (and American) context. With these responses arose an articulated need for a ceremony in which young Catholics choose Catholicism for themselves among all of the religious opportunities afforded them by pluralism in America's "voluntary religious culture." For some, confirmation fit the bill.

During the latter half of the decade, the "ego" and "id" take precedence, in some cases, to the *imago Dei* and the Incarnation as starting points for Christian studies of the human person because of the growing influence of popular psychological theory. This development, too, had its effects on confirmation, which comes to be understood as a time when young Catholics are brought closer to God, away from their alienated selves. This process is primarily an internal one that flowers inside of the human person enabling her to act in the church in a meaningful and mature fashion. Reinforced by the dominant pluralistic social climate, this theology begins to hold serious sway among proposed theologies of confirmation.

Chapter 3

Confirmation and Negotiating Pluralism: 1971–1980

As the council's reforms began to hit the ground in the United States and the first generations of Catholic children were raised outside of the Catholic subculture, Catholic identity was unsettled. What it meant to be Catholic was assumed in the subculture, but identity now needed to be asserted and even reconceived in the context of pluralism.[1] Battles over the proper interpretation of conciliar documents were intertwined with the struggle to find Catholic identity outside of the "ghetto." The younger generation of Catholics was especially looking for some way to be Catholic that was at once distinctive in society, vibrant, and engaging amidst the jostling of liturgical practice and spirituality in general.

Throughout the decade and following, the Catholic charismatic renewal became a major way in which especially younger Catholics asserted their identity as they responded to both postconciliar and post-subculture uncertainties. As the renewal grew in popularity, it too became a major part of the story of confirmation theology in the twentieth century. Some involved in the renewal even adopted confirmation as its centerpiece. This appropriation of confirmation was supported by the theologies of commitment that had developed previously and continued to inform the sacrament's theological and pastoral development in noncharismatic circles. This commitment theology fit nicely with both the goals of the renewal and the newfound need to assert Catholic identity.

26

Some prominent U.S. Catholics cast Catholics' new relationship to the wider culture as a major step in their "maturation" process.[2] That is, leaving behind the subculture made Catholics more mainstream, more adult, more respected, and greater contributors to U.S. culture. This perspective was bolstered by a similar understanding of the new posture of the church in its relationship to the modern world. According to many American commentators on Vatican II, the church had left behind its defensive posture in order to embrace the modern world; it had abandoned childish resistance in favor of mature acceptance. Practicing confirmation as a rite of maturity paired well with this sense among U.S. Catholics. Young people were no longer stuck in a defensive, immature church, but grew into Catholic maturity in a pluralistic culture.

During this period, confirmation also served as a conduit for the larger ecclesiological questions that emerged from the dissolution of the subculture. Confirmation became a stage for the struggle between the more voluntaristic ecclesiology of modernity and the more universal ecclesiology of Catholicism. While "religion" fits into pluralistic societies as a group of voluntary associations, Catholic ecclesiology claims that the church is not simply a group one chooses to be a part of, but rather that one is called by God, perhaps over a long period of discernment, to be a member. The intensity of this struggle was heightened especially due to the dissolution of the subculture. The natural relationship between theologies of sacraments and of the church lends ecclesiological relevance to confirmation theologies, but the ecclesiological tug-of-war during this period all but assured that confirmation theology would see its effects.

The Revised Rite of Confirmation

Shortly after the turn of the decade, Pope Paul VI oversaw the promulgation of the new rite of confirmation called for by Vatican II. The new rite is emblematic of the continued integration of conciliar reforms into Catholic life: there is a clearer articulation of the connection between baptism and confirmation and a renewed emphasis on the Person of the Holy Spirit, an emphasis that permeates the conciliar documents, at least in an incipient way.[3]

The revised rite of confirmation marks the starting point for this period not because it had a sweeping influence over how confirmation theology was done, but because it codified some preconciliar, conciliar, and postconciliar theological movements. While many of the contemporary approaches to confirmation could find expression in the prayers and rubrics of the revised rite, the rite serves as a step further away from the dual emphases characteristic of the Catholic Action period: the distinction between baptism and confirmation and the personal strengthening of the confirmandi.

As mentioned in chapter 2, *Sacrosanctum Concilium* explicitly called for a revised rite of confirmation "so that the intimate connection of this sacrament with the whole of the Christian initiation may more clearly appear" (71). The revised rite expresses this unity of baptism and confirmation by naming confirmation as another step on the path begun at baptism. From the outset, the rite solidifies the unity of baptism and confirmation and identifies confirmation as the sacrament in which Catholics receive the Holy Spirit.[4] In the celebration of the rite itself, the connection to baptism is further expressed in two major ways—the inclusion of a renewal of baptismal vows and the instruction that the rite normally take place within the Mass, "in order that the fundamental connection of this sacrament with all of Christian initiation may stand out in clearer light."[5]

Theologians immediately leading up to and following Vatican II had emphasized the Holy Spirit as Gift over the seven gifts of the Holy Spirit as the special grace of confirmation.[7] The rite responds to this shift. Ralph Keifer, executive secretary for the International Committee on English in the Liturgy (ICEL), writes in 1972, "If anything is clear from the new rite of confirmation, it is the emphasis it places on the Holy Spirit."[8] Indeed, the personal gift of the Holy Spirit is expressed in the celebration of the rite, particularly in the revised formula for anointing with sacred chrism. The rite adopts a fifth-century Byzantine formula for the anointing, a formula best translated into English as, "Be sealed with the gift of the Holy Spirit."[9] These words replace those spoken in the Latin Church since the twelfth century, "I

In *Divinae Consortium Naturae* (DCN), the Apostolic Constitution promulgating the *Rite of Confirmation*, Paul VI writes: "Since the Rite of Baptism for Children, revised at the mandate of the Council and published at our command, is already in use, it is now fitting to publish a rite of confirmation, in order to show the unity of Christian Initiation in its true light. In fact, careful attention and application have been devoted in these last years to the task of revising the manner of celebrating this sacrament. The aim of this work has been that 'the intimate connection of this sacrament with the whole of Christian initiation may stand out more clearly.' But the link between confirmation and the other sacraments of initiation is more easily perceived not simply from the fact that their rites have been more closely conjoined; the rite and words by which confirmation is conferred also make this link clear."[6]

sign you with the sign of the cross and confirm you with the chrism of salvation. In the name of the Father and of the Son and of the Holy Spirit." The effect of this change is clearly to emphasize the Holy Spirit as Gift. The new formula also notably uses the singular genitive *doni*, indicating that there is one Gift, which is the Holy Spirit, from whom all other gifts proceed. The Apostolic Constitution underscores this theology, calling confirmation the sacrament "through which the faithful receive the Holy Spirit as a Gift." Pope Paul's emphasis on the Holy Spirit as personal gift reflects reigning currents in confirmation theology but also seems to gesture ecumenically toward sacramental practice in the East.[10]

Paul VI writes that in both the East and the West, the *anointing* with chrism holds the most significant place in the confirmation ritual. Yet the pope stresses the continuity of confirmation throughout the centuries with *the laying on of hands* in Acts 8. In order to draw these two together, Pope Paul declares that the *anointing itself* "in a certain way represents the apostolic laying on of hands."[12] The new rite no longer prescribes that the celebrant place one hand on the confirmand's head while anointing the forehead with the other, as in the previous rite, yet there is, in the new rite, a separate laying on of hands that the celebrant performs while saying the prayer *prior to* the anointing with chrism. Pope Paul notes that this laying on of hands "is still to be regarded as very important, even if it is not of the essence of the sacramental rite: it contributes to the complete perfection of the rite and to a more thorough understanding of the sacrament."[13] Although the pope appears to be drawing on scholastic distinctions to determine what is absolutely necessary for confirmation to have "happened," his categories are not entirely scholastic, insofar as what "contributes to the complete perfection of the rite" was not a clear scholastic designation. For this reason, theologians debated the pope's purposes in making such a distinction.[14] There was a lively debate about the "essence" of the sacramental rite. However, such sharp distinctions of sacramental matter

Boniface Luykx, former member of the Sacred Congregation for Divine Worship, attests to the importance of ecumenical concerns in the revision of sacramental rites. Luykx discloses that while preparing a different rite—that of baptism of adults—a theological expert in Eastern Church relations "told the commission that the consequences of separating confirmation from baptism and administering it at an adult age would be so serious for the future of [East-West] ecumenical relations that the perspectives of reunion would be irrevocably closed."[11]

and form indicative of the scholastic era are subsumed within the rite's ecumenical trajectory and emphasis on the Person of the Holy Spirit.

Catholics in a Plural Society

Revivification of the Holy Spirit's presence drove the Catholic charismatic renewal. The renewal emphasized the continuity of the church with the Pentecost event and thereby centered on the Holy Spirit's manifest gifts and effects. It began among a few students and professors at Duquesne University in the mid-sixties[15] and grew to be "one of the most dramatic, ecumenical, long-lasting, and widespread spiritual movements of the postconciliar period, touching millions of Catholics between 1965 and 1990."[16] Eventually the renewal reached across national borders, but it began and was most popular in the United States.[17] An outgrowth of ecumenical conversations, the movement had a Pentecostal feel, but remained devotedly Catholic.[18]

The charismatic renewal had a far-reaching influence in the church. Indeed, many twenty-first century Catholics—both clerical and lay—bear its influence. Since, near its inception, confirmation became *the* sacrament of the renewal, it bears some further examination here.

In the post-subculture and postconciliar U.S. Catholic Church, the younger generation of Catholics especially was in search of firm ground on which to set its feet. The outbreak of the Catholic charismatic renewal gave these Catholics a medium to be Catholic in a church torn by arguments about *Humanae Vitae* and liturgical reforms in a society characterized by individualism and pluralism. Reflecting on this era, Debra Campbell writes, "Marriage Encounter, Cursillo, and the Catholic charismatic movement . . . became popular because they responded to the hunger for community and sanctity that was not being satisfied elsewhere in the American Catholic community."[19] Campbell finds fertile soil for the charismatic renewal in the void left by the dissolution of the Catholic subculture, which often included the breakdown of the ethnic and geographical parish structures and broad Catholic entry into the wider individualized, pluralistic culture. In many cases this shift renders parish membership susceptible to a market mentality with its concomitant consumer decision-making processes. In contrast to shifting parish life, the renewal provided consistent Catholic spiritual relationships. As had Virgil Michel and H. A. Reinhold before them, many leaders of the renewal pointed to the debilitating individualism of the dominant culture; in the words of Franciscan and renewal supporter Michael Scanlan, "It is not normal for Christians to live isolated, individualized or alienated lives. One problem today in the Church is that there is so little community—our parishes are so large, strangers sit next to strangers at Sunday Mass."[20] In a wider culture that places a large stake on the individual's achievements, the renewal strives to offer a Catholic subcommunity rooted in the Spirit in which the Christian life—its joys and burdens—is shared.[21]

> "Although Confirmation is sometimes called the 'sacrament of Christian maturity,' we must not confuse adult faith with the adult age of natural growth, nor forget that the baptismal grace is a grace of free, unmerited election and does not need 'ratification' to become effective" (*Catechism of the Catholic Church*, par. 1308).

The renewal found itself at the heart of a cultural struggle that cut to the very heart of the church's understanding of what it means to become a Christian. At the 1978 Priests' Conference on the Catholic Charismatic Renewal, Bishop Lucker of Minnesota identifies both an intra- and an extraecclesial challenge to which the renewal responds. The former is an over-intellectualization of Catholic life; he laments that Catholics "know about Christ and [do] not know Christ" because "logical instruction is taken to be catechesis and vast numbers of Catholics have never been evangelized."[22] The bishop is not alone in his critique.[23] Charismatics often defined the work of the Spirit in contrast to the rational, especially since the latter often had exclusive priority in catechesis. Extraecclesially, Bishop Lucker sees the renewal as responding to the cultural pull on Catholics, which threatens their unique identity. The renewal offers a vibrant way of being Catholic that can perchance stand up to the attractiveness of cultural icons such as Johnny Carson and Las Vegas.[24]

"Baptism in the Holy Spirit"

In response to this struggle, those involved in the renewal pushed for a thoroughgoing revitalization of the formal sacramental life of the church. The ritual practice at the heart of this revitalization was "baptism in the Holy Spirit." In the Catholic charismatic discussion about the baptism in the Spirit, many issues arise that mirror issues in the confirmation discussion, including: the action of the Holy Spirit, the question of individualism, the role of the laying on of hands, and coming to maturity in the Catholic faith. As the renewal strove to respond to the challenges of the wider culture, it addressed many of the same issues that theologians and catechists were trying to address in confirmation more generally. It would be a short step to forge a connection between the renewal and confirmation.

Drawn from Pentecostal traditions, the baptism in the Spirit is understood by Catholic charismatics to bring the graces received in the sacraments of initiation to full effect. Scanlan describes the practice in this manner:

> What millions of Catholics have discovered in the past twelve years is that they can enter into a deeper level of life in the family of God and know a new empowering in the Holy Spirit, through making an act of total commitment to the Lord and inviting the Holy Spirit to take over their lives. This action is what is meant by "being baptized in the Holy Spirit" or by "receiving the release of the Holy Spirit." In one sense, this is not a new dimension of God's life since it is exactly the intention of the sacraments of Baptism, Confirmation, and Eucharist. But, in another sense, it is distinctly empowering and for the great majority of people the most intimate, powerful and transforming spiritual experience in their lives to that point. The result of being baptized in the Spirit is to know a fullness in the relationship of the Family [sic] of God and, most clearly, to know the empowering of the Holy Spirit to live those relationships.[25]

Renewal leaders' emphasis on commitment and on having a profound spiritual experience echoed many of the concerns in recent approaches to confirmation theology. Scanlan connects the baptism in the Spirit to the strengthening of the "family of God," which jibes with his own critique of the individualistic culture. Yet, not all renewal leaders, especially those who wrote during its nascence, shared his ecclesial emphasis.[26]

Pioneers of the renewal at the University of Notre Dame, Kevin and Dorothy Ranaghan, for example, emphasize building a personal relationship with Jesus via baptism in the Spirit. The Ranaghans are clear that there is no prescribed ritual for the baptism in the Holy Spirit, for such uniformity might deny the spontaneous work of the Spirit. Rather, it can happen anywhere, alone, or in community.[27]

In light of perspectives such as the Ranaghans', it seems right to conclude that characterizations of charismatic spirituality as individualistic throughout the first decade of the renewal's existence had some substance and, further, that Scanlan's 1979 book responded to them. This is particularly interesting not only because of the individualistic tones that had begun to be sounded in the confirmation discussion, but also because the movement, at least in one respect, *responds* to the isolation or upheaval that especially younger, energetic Catholics were feeling in a pluralistic culture.

With the laying on of hands a marked component of the confirmation rite, there was some question about what seemed to be the same ritual action in the baptism in the Spirit. Holy Cross Father Edward O'Connor points to agency as the distinguishing factor—the baptism in the Holy Spirit is God's interior work in the heart of an individual and the laying of hands can be done by anyone; therefore the baptism in the Holy Spirit does not equal the laying on of hands.[28] Even with O'Connor's distinction, the association of laying on of hands with the charismatic renewal generally, and with baptism in the Holy Spirit particularly, served as a point of connection between the renewal and confirmation.

The desires that drove commitment theologies of confirmation at the end of the previous period and especially during this period were evident, too, in the discussion about the baptism in the Spirit. For instance, James Byrne, an early renewal leader writes, "It is necessary for every man to make a personal act of faith in Jesus since it is only through him that man can come to the Father. This is done for most Catholics at baptism by sponsors, but it is necessary that when we reach maturity we reaffirm their act of faith and make it our own."[29] Here, the baptism in the Holy Spirit serves as ratification, a personal acceptance of the baptismal covenant at a mature age. The connection between commitment and maturity theologies of confirmation and the mature acceptance of Christ in the charismatic baptism in the Spirit was clearly implicit. Some involved in the renewal made these connections explicit.

Baptism in the Holy Spirit and Confirmation

Especially during the renewal's incipient stages, many involved with the movement strove to keep baptism in the Holy Spirit distinct from the sacraments of initiation in order to bolster, rather than obstruct or supplant the official sacramental life of the church.[30] Others involved in the movement saw obvious connections between the goals of the renewal and some directions in confirmation theology and practice. There were at least five reasons for this correlation. First, the renewal's emphasis on the charisms of the Holy Spirit and confirmation's articulated connection to the Holy Spirit facilitated a theological point of contact. Second, the widespread disagreement over confirmation and its place in the sacramental matrix allowed for open appropriation to particular pastoral circumstances—pastorally, the free-floating age of confirmation fit neatly into the effervescent, revivalist spirit of the renewal. Third, as noted above in Byrne's description, there is a clear sense of an adult commitment to Christ inherent to the theology of the baptism in the Spirit and those voices articulating confirmation as a time of commitment were most prevalent during the beginning stages of the renewal. Fourth, both baptism in the Spirit and postconciliar theologies of confirmation maintained an explicit connection to the sacrament of baptism. Fifth and finally, confirmation and baptism in the Holy Spirit share common Scriptural warrants.[31]

The similarities between his parish's preparation pamphlet for confirmation and his participation in the baptism in the Spirit struck Stephen Clark.[32] This experience drove Clark into further reflection on the role of confirmation. Returning to Scripture, he saw a disjunction between Acts 8 (Peter and John laying on hands in Samaria) and Acts 9 (Paul laying on hands at Ephesus) and confirmation as currently celebrated. When the apostles laid hands on new converts, the converts spoke in tongues and prophesied. Clark writes, "if those who were being confirmed actually started speaking in tongues and prophesying like the disciples at Ephesus did, or if they even just experienced a deep filling and strengthening of the Holy Spirit, everyone would be surprised and wonder what had happened." He concludes that baptism in the Spirit is a renewal of confirmation, that those receiving it are receiving the effects of confirmation, and that "There is no good reason why Christians should not receive the baptism of the Spirit at confirmation."[33]

It turns out that Clark was not the only one suggesting such a connection. In 1971 Robert Wild, a parish priest, published a confirmation program that he had designed in trying to implement some aspects of the renewal. It is not coincidental that Wild's attraction to the charismatic movement and desire to integrate it into his parish community finds particular, seemingly natural expression in the confirmation program.[34] He notes that following confirmation, he handed out to the students a sheet entitled, "What To Do After Confirmation," adapted from the Pentecostal "What To Do After the Baptism (in the Spirit)." Wild explains this connection: "It is a debated theological problem whether this 'baptism in the Spirit,' spoken of in pentecostal circles, should be equated with the sacrament of confirmation. Whether it should or not, for practical, pastoral purposes, there is no reason why we cannot use much of the thinking which surrounds the 'baptism in the spirit [sic]' and apply it to confirmation."[35] While the theological debate rages on, the pastoral link between the two, specifically the reception of the Spirit and the move to maturity of young Catholics seems natural for Wild and Clark.

As these connections became clearer, others argued for a correlation between the two. In another confirmation preparation program, the authors "felt it was vital that the teachers [in the program] should have had the experience of the 'baptism in the Holy Spirit' because this is actually what Confirmation should be."[36] One would assume that the teachers had received confirmation itself! This suggestion moves beyond a mere correlation between confirmation and baptism in the Spirit, to an argument that the latter should be a model for the former, properly celebrated. In one of the sample presentations to the students, the authors explain, "We will speak of Confirmation and baptism in the Holy Spirit—and these will be interchangeable expressions. They mean the same thing." The authors model confirmation on the baptism in the Spirit, explaining the purpose and effects of confirmation as similar to those of the baptism in the Spirit. It is not surprising, then, that they hold that "Confirmation is an introduction to adulthood," a version of a maturity theology. As adults, participants "are individuals, no longer being carried in by their parents as they were on their baptismal day, but now able to stand and say *they* want to commit their lives to the way and the truths of Jesus Christ."[37] Those preparing for confirmation are to choose for themselves whether they are ready to make a firm commitment to living the Christian life. Among these connections between confirmation and baptism in the Holy Spirit, we also see some of the influence of the vast cultural change that Catholics underwent during the previous decade, as there is a sense here that the mature "individual" must, out of the throes of pluralism, commit to full membership in the church.[38]

The effects that Antekeier and the Vandagriffs ascribe to confirmation mirror the less "charismatic" effects of baptism in the Spirit.[39] They discuss a personal and continued encounter with Christ if the confirmandi draw upon the graces of confirmation, a common emphasis of baptism in the Holy Spirit. The authors also advise the young Catholics to "[open] the scripture at random . . . to help you in your daily lives."[40] Many discuss opening the Bible at random as a Spirit-guided practice of the renewal.

Despite all the fervor surrounding the charismatic renewal, there were, of course, some who were critical of the close association of confirmation and the renewal. Notably many of those who reacted against the charismatic element in confirmation also shied away from emphasizing confirmation as a time of mature commitment.[41] Often they do so out of both theological and pastoral concern; for example, Kenneth Smits writes, "Individual Christian commitment is important. But it is not the total goal of Christianity. Christian maturity is good. But there is a maturity appropriate to each age and stage of growth."[42] Smits finds that placing undue weight upon confirmation as *the* sacrament of Christian coming of age or as *the* sacrament of the charismatic renewal is ultimately detrimental to a thorough understanding of the sacrament itself and its role in the context of the entire Body of Christ. Smits argues that an overemphasis on the reception of the extraordinary gifts of the Spirit is both theologically shortsighted and intimidating for the typical confirmand.[43] Smits and others critique confirmation theologies that are too clearly, overtly, and specifically involved in a response to the wider culture either via the charismatic renewal, or the wider move to consider confirmation as the mature, committed choice for Catholicism in the pluralistic context.

Negotiating Pluralism

Theologies of confirmation that emphasize confirmandi's commitment to, and maturity in, their Christian faith were integral to the appropriation of confirmation as the sacrament of the charismatic renewal. These theologies, which emerged during the previous period, picked up steam during the period under consideration here. It is not surprising that they picked up steam in light of this sweeping diagnosis by Anglican liturgist Daniel Stevick, "The meaning of becoming a Christian has been influenced by rationalism, romanticism, the rise of psychology, the reshaping of society and the sensibility to industrialism and technology, and, above all, by the general de-Christianization of the West. . . . With the death of Christendom, the inherited liturgy of Christian initiation has come to appear as a series of isolated ritual events."[44] Arguably, the immigrant culture in the United States provided a kind of "Christian culture" that placed and unified the sacraments of initiation into a congruent whole. It also mitigated the various modern movements and ideas that Stevick mentions. Confirmation, as one of these three sacraments, underwent serious reconsideration in light of the particular social change in the United States.

As Catholics' immersion in pluralism widened and deepened, confirmation theologies and programs continued to reflect the effects of this encounter in a variety of ways. The charismatic renewal's appropriation of confirmation is one example. But there were others. Some confirmation theologies reflected the culture-wide individual and anti-institutional emphasis; some reacted against it. Some, as mentioned above, saw confirmation as the opportunity for young Catholics to elect the church for themselves, committing to it among the available options, and a few reacted against this move. These perspectives have, at their root, both ecclesiological and cultural assumptions that cannot be easily separated. As illustrated in chapter 2, the wider pluralistic culture tends to encourage a more voluntaristic ecclesiology and the degree to which one adopts such an ecclesiology is evident in one's approach to confirmation.

Confirmation, Commitment, and Identity

As Catholic identity became a major concern, especially in a perceived culture of religious indifference, any display of commitment to Catholicism on the part of young people called out for ritual recognition. Often, confirmation fit the bill. Yet sometimes other young people were left out in the cold, a dynamic aptly discussed by Joseph Cunningham, priest of the Diocese of Brooklyn: "In this era of religious indifference, pastors and educators are eager to utilize any legitimate ritual that will recommit young adults to the faith and provide them with a ritual experience to climax ambitious programs of instruction and apostolic activity." In response, Cunningham suggests that confirmation should always be celebrated in the same rite as baptism since "the present ritual of confirmation cannot possibly sustain the weight of responsibility that recommitment and Christian maturity will demand of it."[45] Cunningham finds the Eastern practice of celebrating the sacraments of initiation in infancy more attractive because it better exemplifies the intimate connection between baptism and confirmation expressed in *Sacrosanctum Concilium*.[46] This would only be possible if the ordinary faculty to confirm were given to all priests, yet Cunningham argues that the present alternative is to continue disappointing confirmandi, who come to expect a moving spiritual experience followed by a palpable change in their lives as a result of confirmation and often notice nothing, or at least very little.[47]

It was becoming clear that confirmation needed something, though; its lack of a clear place in Catholic life was only magnified by Vatican II and the revised rite. There were some who thought a newfound, reinvigorated theology lay in fitting confirmation with the cultural need for commitment. Not only would this address a catechetical need, but also breathe new life into an antiquated sacrament. Often, however, these efforts sacrificed important Catholic theological maxims. In his book, *Personal Pentecost*, LaVerne Haas argues that confirmation is the time to celebrate change in the life of an individual. He takes the primacy of the individual person, over and against "any church or institution," as a starting point for his analysis of confirmation.[48] Haas describes confirmation as "a religious event in the life of the individual" that "must confront the person with the presence of the Transcendent." Haas appeals to the general religious experience of every individual, without tradition-specific discrimination. He writes, "When Neanderthal man buried food and weapons with the dead at Wadi el Mughara in Palestine, the event was no less relevant than the Resurrection story. . . . Theologians and churchmen, in religious education, do a disservice to modern religious man when they equate *homo religiosus* with the people of the Old and New Testament. Confirmation today is an example and the result of this short-sightedness." Instead of a peculiarly Christian focus, Haas argues for a more general understanding of confirmation rooted in *"homo religiosus."* In so doing, he shifts the central focus of confirmation from the Holy Spirit as Gift to the human person receiving the gift. He writes, "As a religious event, confirmation focuses upon the relationship between man and deity." He then clarifies, "The structure of confirmation is really triangular—the Transcendent, the community and the self—and as happens in triangles, personal integrity is at times threatened."[49] Haas's proposal for a theology of confirmation is marked not only by the anti-institutionalism of the times, but also by the ecclesiological voluntarism of a pluralistic culture. His triangular structure places the baptized individual outside of the community until she decides to become a mature member. One can see the contrast with an ecclesiological image such as the Body of Christ, where each person is a member of the Lord's body, who nevertheless maintains a particular, important function.

Negotiating pluralism, especially the push toward a more voluntary understanding of church membership, was difficult. Cultural currents cried out for Catholics to find some way to mark their official, mature, voluntary commitment to Catholicism. Confirmation seemed to be the perfect opportunity. Some, such as Bishop Charles Buswell, recognized the demand, but tried to avoid making confirmation *the* moment of commitment.

In a paper presented to the 1971 Diocesan Liturgical Commissions' National Meeting, the bishop of Pueblo argues that "Confirmation is a most appropriate time to emphasize that belonging to Christ's church is a matter of personal decision. . . . This decision, however, must never be relegated exclusively to the sacrament of confirmation."[50] Buswell wants to unburden confirmation of the weight it has begun to carry in

Catholic formation, while still maintaining that church membership hinges on a personal decision, emphasized at confirmation.[51] Buswell responds pastorally to two particular culture-wide situations: (1) "many Catholics continue to see the sacrament as the moment of personal decision regarding their own Catholicism" and (2) "the tendency is growing among some Catholics to take their Catholic heritage lightly."[52] He describes the predicament of Catholic identity in a pluralistic culture well: identity withers away unless it is strongly asserted. But asserting it strongly, especially at a designated moment such as confirmation, has its own drawbacks. The Catholicism of the subculture, whatever its shortcomings, seemed to form and maintain a Catholic identity without the necessity of a particular moment of individual identity assertion.

In response to this problematic, Buswell calls confirmation a time to "reaffirm . . . personal allegiance to the Catholic Church," symbolized by the presence of the bishop.[53] He calls for a confirmation ceremony centered on each individual confirmand. In reaction to an "assembly-line" based ceremony, he writes, "During both catechesis and ceremony, our attention must ultimately center on the individual, not on the large group in front of us."[54] Since confirmation is a time to celebrate the personal decision of this individual, it follows for Buswell that the focus should center on each individual, instead of the organic action of the Holy Spirit in the church.

Bishop Buswell's different starting point—the interconnection of the three sacraments of initiation—leads him to different conclusions than Haas. He strives to maintain a certain integrity for Christian initiation, holding that "the eucharist, not confirmation, is the sacrament of commitment, the covenant sacrament." This important sacramental reality needs emphasis, Buswell argues, in order "to counteract the stress that has been put upon confirmation as the principal sacrament of that precise moment when one decides to be a full-fledged Roman Catholic Christian."[55] Buswell acknowledges confirmation as a time of commitment, not a commitment, however, made in isolation from the rest of the Christian life.

Some responses to the challenges of being Catholic in a culture of choice were more critical of any association of commitment or maturity with confirmation. Ralph Keifer critiques the growing influence of individualistic pluralism on the practice of confirmation and on Catholicism in general. Keifer refers to an event in the summer of 1972 of two hundred thousand young people gathered to "affirm their 'mature commitment to Jesus Christ,'" while exhibiting a lack of concern for social issues.

This "curious spectacle" is, argues Keifer, at best dishonest and at worst a betrayal of the Christian tradition.[56]

Keifer diagnoses the difficulty with confirmation as only a surface symptom of a more serious disease festering in "the primary sacrament, the Church." Like Debra Campbell, Keifer lambastes Catholic parish life in the early seventies, writing, "The modern parish operates like a filling station, where isolated individuals are supposed to take their sustenance from time to time. . . . Instead of an invitation to "come, follow me," we are now urged to "do it yourself.""[57]

Keifer jettisons the idea that confirmation, celebrated as a rite of maturity, will solve the challenge that Catholics face in pluralism. The problem is more fundamentally ecclesial. Without a church that functions as a vibrant "corporate environment," holding its own in the public of "a pluralist, secular society," Keifer argues that Christian maturity is impossible, or at least extremely difficult, to achieve.[58] This palpable lack of "corporate environment" is a void that has not, according to Keifer, been adequately filled since the end of the "old medieval consensus." The Second Vatican Council "was willing to acknowledge its passing" but still "the church has done little to provide a new 'corporate environment' which would allow for a perceptible Christian presence in wider society." He calls neither for an increase in simple social interaction nor for more "sensitivity sessions." This "corporate environment," the establishment of which must precede any serious answer to sacramental questions, must be rooted in concrete, demanding Christian action nourished by prayer. In contrast to Haas and even Buswell, Keifer paints an ecclesiological picture that is "unabashedly sacramental." It is from within this corporate environment that Christians can begin to understand maturity and grow into it.[59]

Beyond his title, one might forget that Keifer's topic is confirmation, but his work attests to the deep-seated cultural and ecclesial difficulties that Catholics faced and considered in light of celebrating confirmation. Keifer argues that before confirmation can even be rightfully considered, Catholics' place in the wider culture needs further clarifying and active restructuring.

Preparing for Confirmation in a Plural Society

The wider pluralistic cultural situation also affected confirmation discernment and preparation. Confirmation not only needed to be oriented toward a personal decision, but needed also to be intelligible to non-Catholics among whom Catholics played, worked, and learned. Another advantage of developing confirmation as a maturity or commitment rite was its ability to make sense to non-Catholics, and especially non-Christians.

Some confirmation programs encourage those discerning the "highly personal decision"[60] of participation in confirmation to seek the advice of the non-Catholics with whom they associate: "We live in a pluralistic society and the students will lead their lives as confirmed Catholics among people who do not necessarily share their vision of life. Therefore, it would be well if the students would find out what some of their non-Catholic friends and neighbors think about their intentions to think seriously about being confirmed."[61] Here, the program builds in concern for the child's wider environment, including non-Catholics. The shift here is palpable; in a subculture-centered Catholicism, such concerns did not even demand consideration. The exercise, in this context, pairs nicely with the idea of confirmation as a maturity or initiation rite akin to other rites of maturity or initiation; for non-Catholics would not be able to comment on Catholic confirmation unless it were presented and understood in a more generalized fashion. If the authors have in mind a conversation with non-Christians, one would be hard-pressed to make sense of confirmation as the Gift of the Holy Spirit apart from specific reference to the New Testament. A maturity rite, however, has myriad secular and religious parallels.

Theologians and pastoral ministers alike debated the role confirmation could play in the new cultural position in which Catholics increasingly found themselves. Looking for the best response to the many religious options in a pluralistic culture, some built out of confirmation an opportunity for and a celebration of young people's "mature" Christian commitment. A few were critical of this move and instead emphasized the role of the Holy Spirit in confirmation and the ongoing formation in the womb of the church. The discussion is, though, also deeply ecclesiological. The former group largely adopts an ecclesiology with a voluntaristic tinge, arguing that confirmation is the time for young Catholics' voluntary choice of Catholicism for themselves. The latter group, which is clearly in the minority, argues that confirmation is a celebration of the Holy Spirit, who animates the universal church and encourages Christian witness rooted in prayer—witness to the wider culture of choice.[62] The tension between a Catholic ecclesiology in which people are called by God to be members of the Body of Christ and a voluntary association model of church, in which individuals choose to come together in common purpose, would endure throughout the rest of the twentieth century.

John Roberto: Maturity and Initiation

In 1978 the landscape of confirmation theology and practice became clear enough (or complicated enough!) for John Roberto in his landmark analysis to trace out two major theological strains running throughout the confirmation discussion in the United States. On one side is "the theological-maturity school," which "view[s] confirmation as a rite of passage, a full commitment to the gospel lifestyle (a recommitment of one's baptism, but now as an 'adult'); a completion of the gift of the Holy Spirit begun in baptism but now brought to its fullness in confirmation." On the other side of the question stands the "liturgical-initiation school," which "views confirmation as a 'solemn pneumatic conclusion to baptism that finally equips one for full sharing in the Eucharistic celebration of a people filled with the Spirit of Jesus whom the Father sent as that peoples' living bond of unity.'"[63] Roberto's project was the first of its kind—a book-length inventory of confirmation theology in the United States. His work is a testament both to the need for a confirmation "roadmap" and the uniqueness of the situation in the United States. Roberto's delineation of the "theological-maturity school" and the "liturgical-initiation school" helped clarify the murky waters of confirmation theology and shape its direction moving into the 1980s.

Many of those examined above would be associated with Roberto's "theological-maturity" school. Confirmation could be closely associated with the charismatic renewal largely because of its viability as a maturity rite. It was this same viability that enabled confirmation, in the context of pluralism, to become the time to choose Catholicism over the other religious options available to the religious "consumer." But there are also those who try to emphasize initiation and choice at the same time; for them, the path to full Christian initiation requires an autonomous choice for Catholicism.

Roberto's "liturgical-initiation school" is shaped heavily by the Rite of Christian Initiation of Adults (RCIA), established in the United States only four years prior to his project. Although nothing significant changed in the rubrics, prayers, and gestures associated with confirmation since the revised rite in 1971, the implications of RCIA influenced the discussion of the sacraments of initiation in general and confirmation in particular.

Many considered RCIA a paradigm for all of Christian initiation. For that reason, three particular aspects of RCIA were significant for confirmation theology after its promulgation.[64] First, the pastor was recognized as the minister of confirmation for adult initiation (whether catechumens or candidates). For some, this opened the possibility that the pastor, instead of the bishop, could serve as confirmation minister on other occasions that also were not emergencies. Since RCIA gestured in this direction, the Eastern practice of initiation (celebrating all three sacraments on one occasion in infancy) received more serious theological consideration.

Second, the order of the sacraments of initiation in RCIA was clear: baptism-confirmation-Eucharist. If, as supposed, RCIA speaks to Catholic initiation in general, many argued, this order should be universal.

Third, some argued for Catholic initiation to be celebrated in adulthood ordinarily. Since RCIA is rooted in the initiation process of the early church (pre-Constantine), with its stages of evangelization, precatechumenate, catechumenate, purification, enlightenment, and mystagogy, some argued from an historical perspective that this process should be universalized. In this case, the normal practice would be to enroll children in RCIA instead of baptizing them as infants (this would also require the pastor to be recognized as ordinary confirmation minister).

Since the source of RCIA lies in relatively pluralistic pre-Christendom Christianity, some saw it as a particularly apt way to deal with initiation in a post-subculture, post-Vatican II, pluralistic situation. The appeals to a "post-medieval church" grow exponentially in the subculture's wake, evidence of the increased feeling of a new social situation for U.S. Catholics during this period. Aidan Kavanagh, a representative of Roberto's "liturgical-initiation school," finds adult initiation particularly effective in pluralism because "We simply cannot depend on evangelization and catechesis being done on youths baptized in infancy by the culture itself, as could a church in thirteenth century Europe." The church's formation program runs counter to the formation of the culture, which, Kavanagh argues, "dehumanizes and dechristianizes youths baptized in infancy more often than not."[65] Kavanagh thinks that Christians who have a conscious memory of their baptism sit in much better stead in this hostile environment. Based on the relationship between Catholics and the wider culture, Kavanagh argues that adult initiation, not infant baptism should be axiomatic Christian practice. In the face of a "largely non-Christian society," Kavanagh finds the catechumenate a more fruitful avenue for Christian formation than baptism followed by catechesis, reaching "commitment" at confirmation.

Roberto, himself convinced of RCIA as a model, also comments on the cultural influence on initiation: "Sociologically, our current pastoral practice relies upon a predominantly Christian culture. Such culture no longer exists and we live in an age of pluralism; and thus there is an urgent need to reestablish a catechumenal structure in which Christians are made."[66] He argues that the church must respond to the pluralistic culture with a more meticulously constructed path for young people, *making* them into Catholics.

Part of Roberto's concern with the cultural situation stems from what he argues is the inadequacy of conflating, without nuance, Thomistic confirmation theology with psychological advances regarding the development of a person. Roberto finds this conflation prevalent in various diocesan regulations that look to the time of "maturity" for the appropriate time of confirmation. The problem, Roberto maintains, is that contemporary psychology is completely foreign to Aquinas's understanding of maturation. Since Roberto identifies this amalgam of psychology and Thomism as "perhaps . . . at the bottom of our confusion," it is not surprising that he sides with the "liturgical-initiation" school.[67] In order to understand this amalgam more fully, it is necessary to examine the development, in this period, of the approaches to confirmation that integrate contemporary psychological theory.

Confirmation and Psychology

As the novelty of psychological theory in catechesis and pastoral ministry began to subside, psychological influences become absorbed into Catholic spirituality and are therefore less explicit in confirmation theology. As we saw in chapter 2, both Mary Charles Bryce and Francis Buckley explicitly cited psychologists, bringing their insights to bear on theologies of confirmation. During this period, the line between what Roberto calls the "psychological understanding" and the "scholastic understanding" is not as clearly defined, resulting in subtler psychological references. That is, the turn to psychology as a form of reaction to neoscholasticism was not the aim of thinkers during this period. Also during this period, some voices arose to critique the manner in which psychology was being adopted in spirituality in general and in terms of confirmation in particular.

Those who find psychological theory a fruitful avenue for thinking about confirmation and catechetical development often argue for confirmation as a rite of maturity for adolescents. The effects of psychological theory are most clearly seen in the structure of preparation programs. Generally speaking, in these programs there is a clear distinction between one's own feelings, positions, or values and those of the church. For example, *Growth in the Spirit* opens with a "value" exercise defined as "something which is important to a person or a community." The note to the parent reads, "This activity is intended to help the students examine *their own* ideas and values. It is *not* intended to present the *objective* values of the Catholic Community."[68] One begins with the personal and moves to the universal, from the inside out as it were. Instead of an explicitly Catholic formation, which would attend to the shaping-ness of tradition, one assumes that the child has been otherwise formed and aims throughout the confirmation program to have the student make her choice.

The aftereffects of the psychological revolution are evident also in starting points for confirmation preparation. Sister Gloriani Bednarski developed her confirmation program after interacting with the youth of her urban parish. Bednarski realized that, "For our young people at this stage in their lives, confirmation could not mean making an adult commitment to Christ and Church; it could not mean arriving at Christian maturity. What it could mean, however, is committing themselves to a new beginning as a new stage in life. What it could mean is the sacramentalizing of a specific 'moment'—the adolescent 'moment.'"[69] Bednarski's program stands as an interesting approach, especially in light of Roberto's study. She pulls apart the mature commitment to Christ theology of confirmation from the psychological insights that bolstered its development. Bednarski takes the stages of psychological development as granted and then proposes that confirmation "sacramentalize" that moment. In the vicissitudes of the culture that Catholic young people inhabit, Bednarski has ruled out a maturity theology of confirmation as it has been elaborated but, instead of moving to a position in Roberto's "initiation school," she places the work of the church in formation on a secondary level and its sacramental life becomes somewhat extrinsic. Confirmation is left as a ritual that marks adolescents' commitment to "beginning a new stage in life." Throughout the program, Bednarski works with the assumption that in order to understand who one is in terms of the church, one must first understand who one is, *tout court*. The latter is aided by understanding the period of adolescence, psychologically.[70] Speaking ecclesiologically, Bednarski gives preference to a voluntary model in which individuals, already formed, come together in community for a common purpose.

Pastor and historical theologian Paul Turner sums up the impact on confirmation of this "evolution in catechetical theory,"

> An environment [of religious formation] which honors personal experience . . . . provided fertile ground for adolescent confirmation. Teens who reflected on their life experience deepened their personal involvement with faith. This they ritualized in a sacrament. Many theologians believed this put more teeth into the sacramental experience, removing its magical tendencies for those who celebrated sacraments without much interior renewal. And educators reflecting on *their* experience with teens discerned that this was a new spirit-filled occasion in the church. They argued that even though the confirmation of teens never existed as a general practice in church history, their experience in the late twentieth century led them to believe that this should be the present and future direction of this sacrament.[71]

Turner, of course, describes the position of those in Roberto's theological-maturity school, positions Turner finds to be linked to a shift in catechetical theory based on contemporary psychological developments.

It is not difficult to sense the frustration in Turner's words. There were, even during this period, scholars critical of the psychological turn largely because it threatens Christianity's particularity. Christopher Kiesling, for example, argues that the move from the general to the specific, that is, from adolescent maturity theory to confirmation challenges the uniqueness of Christian revelation. He writes, "To present confirmation as a sacrament of maturity comparable to the religious rites of passage for adolescents in other societies, religious or secular, risks conveying the idea that Christianity is just a religion, or just another religion."[72] If Turner is correct and adolescent confirmation is intimately connected to this shift in catechetical method based on psychological advances, then Kiesling's critique ultimately is aimed at the psychological shift. He fears that moving from the general category of adolescent maturity and beginning with general psychological human experience will ultimately render Christianity wide open to Feuerbach's critique of religion—that God is simply a projection of our own desires. Instead of Christians identified as children of God, called to be "sharers of the divine nature,"[73] they will be merely associated with all of those who develop a relationship to God "arising out of *man's needs* experienced in personal and social life."[74] The result of such a position is that one chooses one's religion based upon one's perceived personal needs, instead of based on a call from God, akin to those of Abraham, the prophets, John the Baptist, and the apostles. One's perceived personal needs and God's call may not be at loggerheads (although they may be!), but they certainly are not simply identifiable.

Sociologist and theologian Andrew Greeley lays out a more thoroughgoing critique of the widespread popularity of "pop psychology" in Catholic ministry and spirituality.[75] He laments the sloppiness of integrating psychological insights into ministry in an age thirsting for something fresh, new, and impactful: "Catholics discovered sensitivity training and pursued it with all the hunger of those who desperately needed an eighth sacrament because their confidence was woefully undermined in the other seven."[76] As we have seen, in many cases theologians and catechists looked to confirmation as the sacrament to be adapted to the new needs of Catholics in the United States because of that sacrament's own theological homelessness. Pop psychology served as another avenue to pursue confirmation's meaning in the contemporary context. In cases where this was pursued without painstaking care, the confusion identified by John Roberto as arising from the conflation of scholastic theology and psychological theory, resulted.

Greeley offers some examples, "We don't do penance anymore, rather we, 'understand what we are doing'; we are not reborn again through the grace of the Holy Spirit, we rather renew our commitment to our life project. . . . Therapy groups replace worship, encounter weekends substitute for retreats, sensitivity training replaces contemplation . . . Freud has not substituted for Jesus, but Jesus begins to sound very much like Freud."[77] He cites the over-zealous cultivation of critical faculties in seminaries—especially when it comes to Scriptural exegesis—as one root cause of the turn to pop psychology. Graduate school had alienated priests and pastoral ministers from traditional language and symbols and pop psychology served as a suitable replacement. This substitution made sense because of the hot existential movement in Europe, often received in the U.S. as an emphasis on individual personal growth. Greeley writes, "In the wake of the Freudian revolution, self-conscious pursuit of the personal growth of the individual and the fulfillment of human potentialities became the over-riding concern. Wave after wave of pop psychological fads washed up on the shores of American culture, and the intellectual and cultural elites, instead of serving their appropriate role as critics of the new fadism [*sic*], strove to be one step ahead of the masses in discovering what the latest psychological gimmicks were."[78] The confirmation discussion had spread across a notable number of theologians, catechists, and others during this period and confirmation preparation became one of the clearest places of pop psychological influence. The primacy of individual personal growth suited the emphasis on maturity and commitment at the time of confirmation. Greeley affirms a natural affinity between Christianity and psychology, but calls for a more carefully established harmony between the two.

By the end of this period, it was clear that pluralism had changed the context of the confirmation discussion in general and of catechesis in relation to it, in particular. In a bit of a confused shoulder shrug, the 1979 National Catechetical Directory resigned itself to acknowledge, "Practice in this matter [confirmation] now varies so much among the dioceses of the United States that it is impossible to prescribe a single catechesis for this sacrament."[79] The roots of this deep variation rest in a variety of factors. *Quam Singulari* holds some of the responsibility, but so do the variety of other factors discussed in chapters 1 and 2. In this period, confirmation is espoused by proponents of the charismatic renewal and opponents of it, elaborated upon by those that welcome the voluntary ecclesiological emphases of a pluralistic culture with open arms and by those who stand deeply critical of it. The nuances and particulars of these positions, however, even extend beyond the helpful twofold diagnosis of John Roberto. The array of strategies for reaching young people and maintaining theological consistency are illustrated across this period. Nevertheless, we have seen how those who grant too much to psychological categories or to the dictates of life in pluralism jeopardize the very integrity of confirmation as an act of the church, which strives to form members in its fold.

This ten-year period can be summarized as a time of searching out a wide variety of options for response to Catholics' new cultural position. What remains intriguing, and has, I hope, been adequately demonstrated, is how confirmation functions as a sacramental cipher onto which various ecclesiological, pedagogical, and pneumatological concerns can be inscribed. The next, and final, chapter will illustrate how more recent confirmation theology and practice draws upon the work of previous periods and adopts appreciable individualistic and autonomous tones that had been only moderately perceptible in those previous periods.

Chapter 4

Confirmation Theology and Practice: After 1981

As Catholics became socio-economically indistinguishable from their fellow U.S. citizens, confirmation theology focused less upon the formative character of the sacrament and more upon the recognition of an individual's choice and accomplishment. This shift began toward the end of the previous period and becomes widespread over the next decades when Catholics' emergence from the subculture cannot be described as anything but complete. In the ongoing attempt to find a suitable theology for confirmation, catechists' and theologians' emphasis on maturity and commitment developed into marking confirmation as *the* time to choose Catholicism for oneself. Earlier in the century, confirmation had become *the* sacrament of Catholic Action or of the liturgical movement or of the charismatic renewal; in this period, however, confirmation becomes *the* sacrament of Catholic choice.

Choice and Its Discontents

The centrality of "choice" in American self-understanding hardly needs to be argued. From its inception, the U.S. has been understood as the land of the free in contrast to those bound up in tyranny. What Westerners (especially Americans) mean by "freedom" is "choice" or, as it has been put by first-year students of mine, "being able to do whatever

you want." To put it a tad more eloquently, the history of this country involves the gradual deepening, and further understanding, of the maxim
"one person, one vote." Further, the strong emphasis on free-market
economics as the best way to understand how people act brings "religion" into the marketplace as another commodity that is best assimilated
by individual choice. One makes a responsible choice by good market
research of the wide variety of viable choices. The more choices, within
reason, the better. Freedom, again, is the ability to have, and to choose
from among, those options. It could be said that championing this particular understanding of freedom is the one thing that bonds Americans
together.

In light of the overriding argument of this book—that confirmation
theology and practice change to reflect shifts in the relationship between
Catholics and the wider U.S. culture—the centrality of choice in confirmation is not surprising. Catholic formation in a pluralistic context
is difficult. Young people often find the array of theological positions
confusing or, worse, simply a din to which they respond with apathy.
An opportunity for strong, individual assertion seems necessary. Confirmation, with its fluid theology, seems to be the appropriate occasion
to make the choice for Catholicism.

Of course, deep commitment to a religious tradition differs from
consumer choice in a variety of ways. Most notably perhaps is the communal, gradually formative, embodied practice required by the former
in contrast to the more fleeting engagements of the latter. Not sufficiently
attended to, these differences produced some unintended effects. Shortly
following this rather stark emphasis on confirmation as time of choice
during this period and, seemingly all of a sudden, many in the church
began to notice that confirmation became a doorway, not to richer and
perduring engagement with the church, but to exit from church life.
Catechists heard such exclamations as "I memorized everything" or "I
got my sacraments," as confirmandi walked out the doors of the church
not to be seen again. Confirmation became "graduation."

In this chapter we shall see how these two phenomena—pinning
the choice for Catholicism on confirmation and confirmation as "graduation"—are closely related, indeed the former leads to the latter. This
causal relationship underscores what is counterintuitive for the theologians and catechists who promote confirmation as choice. Designating
confirmation as the specific time to choose Catholicism does not solve
the multifaceted problems of forming Catholics in a pluralistic culture.
Sometimes, it even has the opposite effect.

As is clear from the rite itself, the Holy Spirit is associated with confirmation in a unique way. And at least as early as Paul's epistles, the Holy Spirit has been associated with Christian freedom. However, the freedom found in living life in the Spirit is about far more than "choice." After illustrating the shift to a confirmation theology centered on choice and the reaction to it, we shall explore this understanding of freedom in chapter 5 and how it contrasts with individual choice.

Individualism and Pluralism

Many U.S. Catholic historians over the past few decades have pointed to the individualism that has taken a deep hold on Catholics' sensibilities. Though divergent in their ideas about its genesis, extent, and value, Catholic historians are largely in agreement about the gravity of its presence as well as its connection to pluralism. Evaluating the context in 1989, American Catholic historian Jay Dolan identifies economic and educational factors as primary, "Since the 1930s Catholics have climbed up the educational and economic ladder and now rank alongside or ahead of most Protestants. Such change has produced a large dose of individualism among priests, sisters, and lay people. It has also created a great deal of diversity among Catholics; the homogeneity of the past has vanished, swept aside by a rage for pluralism."[1] Pluralizing forces were not simply something "outside" that Catholics had to negotiate in the latter part of the century, but as Dolan points out, Catholics themselves became more pluralized. As different as the Catholic subculture might have been from Boston to Philadelphia to Butte there was a shared Catholic ethos, what Dolan calls "homogeneity," that set Catholics apart from other citizens. As more Catholics were educated in public schools and took white-collar jobs, that distinctiveness faded. Catholic CPAs began to have more in common with non-Catholic CPAs than Catholic meat cutters. This difference obviously influenced the next generation.

Catholic youth were faced with a much different experience of Catholicism than their parents' from both sides. On the one hand, cultural impressions of Catholics as backward and un-American had subsided after World War II and, on the other, Catholicism itself was more stratified and plural. Both sides came to accept Catholicism as a legitimate "religion" among the viable American options, and that acceptance had unintended consequences as David O'Brien, another historian of American Catholicism, points out,

> Rarely noticed . . . is the religious culture to which Americans have adapted, perhaps over-adapted. It is marked (1) by individualism, and thus by an emphasis on religious experience; (2) by pluralism and thus by an emphasis on evangelization, "selling God" and personal decisions, consumer choice, and (3) by voluntary communities, congregations, and thus by fragile structures of ecclesiastical authority and theological orthodoxy. This is the religious culture that was kept partially (and only partially) at bay by Catholic subcultural strategies grounded in the immigration experience.[2]

Eleven years after Dolan noticed individualism and "a rage for pluralism" growing among Catholics, O'Brien echoes those concerns and adds a third: voluntarism, or religious choice. The primacy of individual religious experience paired with ecclesial voluntarism makes the sacramental life of the church simply an add-on to profound religious experience, a second-order choice rather than a conduit for such experiences. Precisely because "religion must be a matter of personal conviction and free choice. . . . Catholic wisdom about sacrament and liturgy, solidarity and organic social obligation that precedes and grounds personal choice is hard to grasp."[3] As O'Brien makes clear, the Catholic imagination, with the sacraments at its heart, grounds personal choice in a rich social context in which young people gradually come to understand their decisions, obligations, and the impact of both. At bottom, the sacramental life of the church is not about an individual's choice; however the cultural environment would lead us to believe that it is.

In my own experience as a classroom instructor, I have had the hardest time trying to get first-year students to understand the nature of a "tradition"—that it is made up of many people over generations, and is composed of practices that change within the tradition, but are nevertheless handed down. Inevitably, there are more than several students who insist upon talking about "my own personal tradition," something that they've culled from elements of all the options available.

The Catholics who were raised in the 1970s and 80s have been particularly affected and formed by this culture. In the whirlwind of choices, decisions, and commitments to be made, these Catholics seem to need a clear occasion to choose their Catholicism. A study published in 1996 describes this generation of Catholics. "Post-Vatican II Catholics [those who grew up in the '70s and '80s] . . . stress the volitional aspects of being in the church—the need to make a personal decision to be Catholic, and the individual's need to choose his or her own religious beliefs and lifestyle."[4] An even greater emphasis on volition abides in the millennial generation, which pairs it with a reticence to make any particular religious choice in favor of an increased religious individualism, a *de facto* satisfaction with pluralism as such in which various elements can be incorporated into one's own "spirituality."[5]

Catechists and theologians responded to the complex problematic of forming young people in this cultural milieu by identifying confirmation as the best time among the sacramental celebrations to express individual choice. Some had treated confirmation as a rite in which *the community* affirms young people's mature place within it. In this period, the choice is inverted—young people choose Catholicism—reflecting the pluralism that O'Brien references, in which all people need an opportunity, even a formal one, to choose their religion. The inversion is a symptom of what O'Brien calls "over-adaptation."

Some confirmation programs published during this final period begin with the premise that confirmation is the time young people choose Catholicism because their authors are convinced by the merits of the voluntary religious culture. Thomas Zanzig is, however, not so convinced. His attempt to broaden the confirmation question is right on the mark: "The real issue we are confronting . . . is the current condition of the church as it struggles to initiate and then nurture the faith of anyone, regardless of age."[6] The question of formation and that of confirmation cannot really be separated, especially during this period. As questions of Catholic formation change dramatically, confirmation is often identified as a prime site of the church's failure and a tweaked approach presented as the answer. While Zanzig is correct, the young, nevertheless, receive particular attention because of their vulnerability, accessibility, and symbolic charge.

Confirmation as Response to Culture

Unsure of the sacrament's ability to stand as a sign of contradiction in the wider culture—representing what O'Brien calls "Catholic wisdom"—and unable to rely upon the catechetical substance of the Catholic household, theologians and catechists needed to find a way to explain confirmation in this new context.

Choice in Pastoral Writings

The challenges of forming young people in pluralism were felt deeply on the pastoral level. The way that confirmation could respond, many aver, is by an increased emphasis on the volitional aspects of the sacramental celebration. Often, this meant delaying confirmation until Catholics have reached a certain age or a certain level of maturity. If, the argument goes, we are able to give young Catholics real agency in the context of confirmation, then we will see a blossoming of Catholic practice among them. While trying to avoid an individualism that would prompt an exit from parish life, they often do not address the interconnection between individualism and voluntarism. Narrowly designating confirmation as the sacrament of choice forces a decision that cannot always be made at a particular time. What is intended to be the culmination of initiation becomes simply the end of participation in parish life. The result was that confirmation became a time of "graduation" from active Catholicism or a "rite of exit" from church life.[7]

When catechist Dan Grippo considers confirmation in terms of the changing structure of the Catholic nuclear family and the conspicuous absence of teenagers in parish life, he concludes, "Because they have developed a stronger sense of their own personal identity, teenage Catholics are ready to meet and appreciate the person of Jesus. . . . For those who do stay with their high-school confirmation program, their confirmation would mean a great deal more to them. They would be *choosing* confirmation, and their choice would affect the rest of their lives. Their future in the church would be marked by personal conviction, not parental or social expectation."[8] Grippo even shifts the agency of the verb "confirm," swapping its traditional subject and object. It is not Christ, the Holy Spirit, or the church (via the bishop) that confirms the baptized, as had been the case at least as early as St. Ambrose, but rather the young person who confirms her choice of the church.[9] Grippo makes extensive use of the pop psychological developments discussed in chapters 2 and 3. He considers, for example, a strong sense of "personal identity" a prerequisite for meeting and appreciating the person of Jesus. Here, the individual's agency is the conduit for greater commitment to Catholicism.

With Grippo's solution, and those like it, the church maintains its role in education, preparing young people for the sacrament

> For St. Ambrose, Christ is the agent who confirms: *Signavit te Deus Pater, confirmavit te Christus Dominus* (God the Father has sealed you and Christ the Lord has confirmed [or strengthened] you). St. Ambrose was also the first one to use the term *confirmavit* to describe the postbaptismal anointing. Shortly thereafter, "confirmation" came to designate the final anointing of the baptismal rite performed by the bishop on a separate occasion when he was unable to be in attendance at the baptism. "Confirmation" also described the Holy Spirit's strengthening of the faithful in the anointing.[10]

even as the confirmand ultimately "confirms" his place in it. Other cate-chists push further in an individualistic direction. In addition to calling confirmation a time of individual choice, they also, somewhat ironically, downplay the church's preparatory role in favor of the interior, spiritual choices of the individual.

Joseph Moore's aptly-titled *CHOICE* program aids high-schoolers in making a "firm personal choice." The process "recognizes the fact that we are dealing with the level of faith of very unique individuals. . . . It recognizes that some young people are at a point where they are able to "confirm" their own baptism and still others may not yet be able to do so. . . . The CHOICE process professes profound respect for the indi-vidual young person and his or her capacity and right to make choices relative to faith and spirituality."[11] *CHOICE* outlines a two-year prepara-tion for confirmation which nobly jettisons sacramental coercion. Yet in order to do so, it espouses a type of individualism in which real spiritual development occurs only from forces inside of the person. The ecclesial dimension, the dimension of the church's continual acceptance and nurtur-ing of all of its children—whether they can admit their surety in the lifelong process of spiritual consolation and desolation at any particular point or not—is underemphasized. Isolating confirmation as *the* time for choice undergirds the individualism in Moore's *CHOICE*. The title is meant to stress the volition of the young person, but there are hints of a voluntaristic ecclesiology, a church of the choosing, that runs throughout the manual.

In this period, generally, catechists and youth ministers are unsure about how to address the ecclesiological dimensions of confirmation. The tensions of cultural voluntarism, Protestant congregationalism, and Catholic universalism pose difficult ecclesial questions embedded in con-firmation theology and preparation. The move to emphasize a veritably autonomous choice in confirmation leans, not surprisingly, toward a heavily voluntary ecclesiology, although many catechists express misgiv-ings about adopting those ecclesiological assumptions full-on.

Steven R. Hemler is a marked exception, who holds no such misgiv-ings. He is rather explicit about laying out a voluntaristic ecclesiology.[12] Yet, his approach is not uncomplicated. Even while adopting a voluntaris-tic ecclesiology, Hemler critiques celebrating confirmation as *the* moment of choice because it often fails in long-term formation: "Given the secular society in which we live, the church cannot assume that those baptized as infants will grow into faithful, committed adult Christians. There is a real need today for the church to do all it can to foster and celebrate mature, committed Christian faith. There are too many nominal 'Sunday only' and

Pelagianism emphasizes the human ability to attain salvation, thus subordinating the priority of God's grace. It was condemned as a heresy in 431 AD at the Council of Ephesus.

inactive Catholics for the church to continue business as usual. There needs to be more committed Christians if the kingdom of God is to grow in our secular, humanistic society."[13] Well made, Hemler's point puts a finger on the tensions surrounding confirmation. He confirms Zanzig's point that the larger question of forming Catholics is played out on the stage of confirmation. Yet, Hemler assumes that confirming self-selecting adults will solve the problem of formation without addressing the inherent problems of a build-up to the particular moment of confirmation. Good catechesis is, of course, very important. If, however, the burden of the growth of the kingdom of God is placed entirely on catechesis, the danger of Pelagianism is real. We cannot simply make ourselves or others into Christians. Only God can do that, with our participation. Room must be made for the efficaciousness of the sacrament and the Holy Spirit's work in the church, particularly in the sacraments. What Hemler and Zanzig do not emphasize is that cultivating openness to the grace of the sacraments must remain a central component to sacramental preparation if we are not to drift into a completely voluntaristic ecclesiology.

Trying desperately to find a solution to the problem of formation in a pluralistic context is a common thread across pastoral writings during this period. But the reflection is not always explicitly cognizant of the uniqueness of the contemporary context. Some appeals to church history anachronistically project the complex of religious pluralism, individualism, and voluntarism upon the early church. One particular catechist describes early Christians as having "searched for a religion, a community, whose beliefs and values they could affirm in their own journey of faith."[14] Early Christians lived with a different cosmological understanding—one without Immanuel Kant's famous distinction between "facts" and "values" and the heavy modern emphasis on the lone searching individual—and as such did not necessarily approach "religion" as lonesome modern individuals searching for a set of "values they could affirm in their own journey of faith." Indeed the very word "religion," in the sense here used, does not enter discourse until the modern period. Whereas the initial moves to make confirmation the sacrament of Christian commitment, and then Christian choice, were hyper-conscious of the uniqueness of the contemporary context and explicitly attempted to respond to it with catechesis and confirmation, by the nineties that context appeared to be simply "the way things are." What O'Brien calls

Catholics' "over-adaptation" to American religious culture manifests it-self in confirmation reflection as that culture is taken as norm. What was an ad hoc response in the late seventies became far more full-throated.

In fact, as the cultural context became more individualized, maturity the-ologies took on its accompanying voluntaristic cast. It seemed only logical for Dominican Frank Quinn to call confirmation, in the twentieth century, an "ersatz bar mitzvah," emphasizing the maturity and adulthood aspects of that analogy.[15] In U.S. culture, though, "choice" is itself constitutive of adulthood or maturity. Maturity only comes when one can choose one's oc-cupation, one's companions, and one's religion for oneself. Any distinction between maturity and choice is very difficult to maintain. Jewish culture and practice are theoretically different. A bar/bat mitzvah occurs at the ap-propriate age whether a ritual is celebrated or not. Age, not ritual, enjoins responsibility under the Law for the thirteen- or twelve-year-old. Whether or not bar/bat mitzvahs have been subject to the same influences as confirma-tion is another study, but for confirmation, a shift to emphasizing maturity during this period is concomitant with a shift to emphasizing choice.

Choice in Sacramental Theology

If marking confirmation as the time of a personal choice for Catholicism appeared to make good pastoral sense, it also had much theological support, especially from mainstream sacramental theologians—those whose books on the sacraments were most often used in the courses that trained parish ministers—who wrote during this period.

Among these theologians, there is agree-ment that those who do the sacrament's "con-firming" are the confirmandi themselves. Further, confirmation is itself necessary only because Catholics baptize infants, a practice most find to be in conflict with the church's early history. Not surprisingly—in terms of confirmation's twentieth-century history—contemporary American experience and per-ceived needs are the driving forces of these theologies. Ray Noll is one of a number who call for a rite of enrollment in long-term baptismal preparation for children, not for

A relatively representative survey of syllabi from courses taught on sacraments in U.S. Catholic graduate programs including Fordham University, Boston College, University of Dayton, Providence College, The Catholic University of America, Marquette Univer-sity, Georgetown University, St. Louis University, University of San Francisco, Washington Theological Union, Graduate Theological Union, University of Notre Dame, and Weston Jesuit School of Theology revealed that at least one of the texts of Ray Noll, Joseph Martos, and Bernard Cooke appeared on more than 85 per-cent of the respondents' syllabi well into the last decade.

parents who have no intention of raising their children Catholic, but rather for those "very dedicated Catholic parents, products in many instances of Catholic high school and Catholic university, who explicitly wish to guarantee their offspring a freedom that they themselves did not have, namely the freedom to choose to be baptized and when." He reflects on the uniqueness of the U.S. cultural situation that informs the desire for this freedom, "In fact, this might not even be an issue in many countries of the world, but for very freedom-conscious Catholics in North American parishes the freedom issue means a lot."[16]

For Noll, the wide variance of confirmation practice is a direct consequence of the separation of confirmation from baptism in the early church.[17] Noll identifies two positions on confirmation in the current conversation that are largely of the same school—both are about commitment—those who think the sacrament should be celebrated in early adolescence and those who think that it should be celebrated some time during the high school years. The key question is when a commitment or "confirming" can be intelligibly made. He thinks that these disagreements "will probably always be with us."[18] Noll's understanding of confirmation and the necessity of designating a time for choice—in proxy of a baptismal choice—seems to belie the Gregory Baum-inspired reflection Noll offers at the end of *Sacraments* in which he describes the church's ministry of word and sacrament analogously to a mother forming a child in symbol and language.[19] Confirmation, considered in this manner, does not fit the analogy. A mother does not normally provide a specific, designated time in which the child can reject or accept her. If the former happens, it happens painfully and often sadly, but not on a prescribed occasion.

Joseph Martos's *Doors to the Sacred* is another text that emphasizes the role of choice in confirmation. The history of the sacraments has become fare in university courses on the sacraments since its first publication in 1981. Martos finds a deep rift between, on the one hand, the official theology of confirmation (expressed in the rite of confirmation and in the 1992 *Catechism of the Catholic Church*) and, on the other hand, Westerners' experience.[20] Unlike Noll, Martos gives a thorough appraisal of the wide variance in confirmation thought and practice in the West. He argues that the predominant understanding of confirmation is rooted in maturity; it is a "communal recognition that those who are confirmed have personally accepted the faith that was once accepted for them, and it is an ecclesiastical call for them to take up the responsibility of being adult disciples of Christ in the world."[21] Martos is explicit about the tension between his theology and the "official theology," but there is a further tension with the *Catechism* that Martos does not explicitly identify. Paragraph 1308, which Martos does not cite, says that confirmation should not be considered a sacrament of baptismal ratification which renders baptism nonefficacious.[22] Martos's reading of confirmation seems to make it a rite of ratification, at least in practice if not in theory. It does so, however, in the service of the cultural shift that U.S. Catholic historians have identified. Confirmation is a recognition, albeit communal, that the individual has personally accepted the faith.

Martos identifies the sacramental theology of another prominent theologian of this period, which fits under Martos's general designation of "doors to the sacred." His analysis of Bernard Cooke's work sounds strikingly similar to Martos's own approach in a 1992 article.[23] He writes, "Psychologists . . . tell us that there are basic human experiences that we all have, and the meanings we attach to them consciously or unconsciously shape our image of ourself [*sic*] and our picture of reality. . . . For Cooke, the purpose of the sacraments is to transform the meaning of those fundamental human experiences."[24] These experiences, Cooke's starting points, have a flavor that is particularly indicative of U.S. culture.

In *Sacraments and Sacramentality*, arguably one of the most important books of the past twenty-five years in sacramental theology in terms of widespread use, Cooke develops not only theologies of the seven sacraments, but he does so in light of a theology of sacramentality that shapes life in general. This sacramental worldview is, for Catholics, overlaid onto basic human experiences, transforming them. The seven sacraments, then, are formal, ecclesial instances of this larger sacramental process.

Cooke treats confirmation in a brief two and a half pages. After noting the liturgical reasons for either placing confirmation in between baptism and First Eucharist or for making confirmation one rite with baptism, Cooke finds "good pastoral reasons for having confirmation at a later age, when the young person can knowingly and freely choose Christian faith." He concludes,

> There seems to be no reason liturgically, theologically, or pastorally, why more than one liturgy could not be celebrated as confirmation of the baptismal choice—perhaps the age of seven or eight, where children really need to choose among the competing values they are exposed to; perhaps again at the beginning of adolescence, when lifestyle and involvement with one or other peer group can be decisive for the years ahead; perhaps again when the young person stands

on the threshold of adult life. Each of these moments of passage occurs after a period of considerable change in experience and at the
beginning of a risky new period.[25]

Cooke avoids designating one moment as the time at which a young
Catholic chooses his faith for himself. He instead calls for repeated con-
firmations "of the baptismal choice." As we have seen before, the subject
of "confirm," for Cooke, is the individual confirmand. The "moments of
passage" that Cooke identifies as appropriate times for this confirming ring
clearly of the pluralism and voluntarism David O'Brien describes. Cooke's
theology of sacramentality sets him up to respond to this cultural shift in a
particular way. Young people are having experiences based on their new
place in the wider culture; Cooke's approach to confirmation, allowing
for multiple celebrations, shifts to reflect these new cultural situations.

In the preceding approaches to confirmation, whether germinated in
a primarily pastoral or theological context, "choice" plays a significant
role. As many would be quick to note, the emphasis on choice alone
does not necessarily give these approaches to confirmation the individualist, pluralist, or voluntaristic edge that Dolan, O'Brien, and others
have found indicative of the culture into which Catholics have been
fully assimilated by this final period of the twentieth century. Designating a particular time for this choice and implying that those who have
chosen Catholicism for themselves are the true members of the church
does, however, tend toward individualism and voluntarism. Among
the positions here considered, a recurring theme has been designating
confirmation as the particular time to make such a choice. Confirmation
provides the young person an opportunity, defined narrowly, to affirm
or "delay" their choice for the Catholic faith.

Laments and Warnings

Designating confirmation as the time of "choice" has, its supporters
argue, the advantage of increasing serious commitment among Catholics.
Pastoral experience, however, seems to point to the opposite outcome—
a drop off in church participation—when confirmation is practiced in
this manner. After widespread adoption of a confirmation theology that
emphasizes the confirmand's choice, many catechists voice concerns
about keeping contact with young people after confirmation. It seems
that wedding one's choice for Catholicism to a designated time unwit-

tingly encourages drifting away after the choice is made because, in the perception of the young person, the hard work has been accomplished once the decision has been made. Confirmation programs with this particular emphasis are often situated in the context of a graduation either from elementary/middle school or from high school, contributing to this definitive break. A second problem with celebrating confirmation as a time of choice is that the practice usually underemphasizes the lifelong development of a relationship with God in the church. This is connected to what O'Brien identifies as individualistic experientialism. If one has already made a choice for Catholicism, then doubts and crises of faith become not integral to the life of faith, but indications that one has made the wrong choice or worse, that God has not held up God's end of the bargain.

Many religious educators were left in the wake of confirmation practiced as a time of choice and scrambling to develop alternative ways to get young people involved. One educator describes his struggle to reinvigorate a parish religious education program after confirmation marked a decisive break between young people and religious education. He and his colleagues nicknamed confirmation "The Sacrament of Exit."[26] An assistant director of religious education (DRE) in Pittsburgh ruefully looks in the mirror, "Perhaps we catechists have contributed to the 'confirmation as graduation' syndrome by preparing candidates as if our program were the last opportunity for them to grow in the faith."[27] This latter educator develops pedagogical techniques for integrating confirmation preparation into the whole of religious education. As we have seen, the problem is not simply tied to education but reinforced by theology as well.

Those who see the difficulties with celebrating confirmation as a time of choice are themselves in a difficult position. Catechists who have inherited the practice of confirmation in its early teen/adolescent form are left to reflect on why young people are no longer involved in the church after confirmation. Parish priest Thomas Taylor's lament, "How can we motivate our young people to a serious commitment to their faith?"[28] encapsulates the collective struggle of catechists trying to reach young Catholics.

The burden of confirmation as "rite of exit," however, seems more appropriately placed on the theology and practice of confirmation that these catechists have inherited, rather than on some sudden lack in catechetical methods. In the first three periods, these theologies have attempted to negotiate the gap between U.S. culture and Catholicism. In this final period, when by all accounts that gap ceases to exist, confirmation itself reflects American individualistic voluntarism. Taylor's solution—making the time of celebration plural and subjective—can only, from this vantage point, reinforce the difficulties.

Into the nineties many catechists are still trying to address the very same difficulty—young people seem well-prepared for confirmation, celebrate it joyously, and then disappear. Lenore Danesco, a DRE from Massachusetts, conveys some of the agony: "Even as we share the joy of confirmation with our young people, there is that nagging question: when will we see them again? We know that confirmation marks a turning point, and that now we must allow our young adults to shoulder responsibility for the faith they have confirmed. But we don't want them to turn away!"[29] Danesco, as well as many others, fail to address the deeper issue, instead accepting the theology of confirmation as a time of choice, and developing educational stopgaps. As have others, Danesco identifies the agent of "confirm" as the confirmand. In this schema confirmation is a committed choice that involves a ratification of baptismal promises and therein assumes that fuller participation in Catholic life will follow. Danesco's educational proposals do not address the individualism that confirmation reinforces when celebrated in this manner.[30] Even those who see a distinction between the vocation of the Christian life and "secular consciousness," struggle to impart this to their students while presenting confirmation as the time to choose Catholicism from among the available religious options.[31]

In 2004, the United States Conference of Catholic Bishops (USCCB) issued a resource guide for bishops on confirmation that warns of approaches to confirmation celebration that emphasize "appropriating faith for oneself" and preparation programs that set up confirmation as a "reward" for catechetical involvement.[32] The resource guide stands in striking contrast to Bishop Roger Mahony's 1981 statement[33] and expresses different emphases than Archbishop William Levada's 1996 theological piece.[34] Where Mahony explains confirmation as a personal act of faith at an appropriate time, the USCCB warns of understanding confirmation as a time when young people take on faith for themselves and is wary of celebrating confirmation at the time when it could be understood as a prize for completing a catechetical program. Levada had suggested that confirmation might be an appropriate time for young people to express their genuine commitment to the church. The resource guide seems to paddle against that current. The hesitation of the resource guide makes sense in light of the obstacles faced by catechists. Rather than attributing this hesitation to pressure from Rome, it seems more likely that the bishops were seeing the pastoral results in the United States of confirmation theologized as the time of personal choice.

USCCB-recommended confirmation preparation materials offer warnings about the "maturity" approach. Many are explicit about continuing the learning process after confirmation. Margaret Hanrahan writes in *Celebrating Our Faith*, "For many young people becoming an adult in the church might mean they have completed learning about their faith. In reality, confirmation should deepen our understanding of and participation in our Catholic faith and community."[35] Another catechetical text, after offering a brief historical overview of confirmation, warns that a theology of maturity does not mean the end of participation in the church.[36]

These catechetical materials address the situation in which dioceses find themselves. For example, in a 2005 report to the diocesan presbyteral council, a committee on the age of confirmation in the Diocese of Lafayette, Louisiana identifies some of the same difficulties in its confirmation programs. The committee lists the following among "perceived weaknesses of current confirmation preparation programs":

- Strong influence of secular culture on confirmands

- Emphasis on confirmation as "Sacrament of Maturity"; maturity in secular culture arrives in 20s or 30s

- Lack of involvement of confirmands and their families in parish life

- Disappearance of confirmands and their families after confirmation.[37]

The committee recommends that these problems be addressed in any diocesan restructuring of the confirmation program.

In the latter part of this period, some theologians also raised a critical voice against theologies of confirmation centered on choice. Some, such as German Martinez, are concerned about the primacy of the pedagogical over and above the sacramental. Martinez argues that, based on the 1971 revision of the rite, confirmation's identity is found in its intimate connection to baptism as a sacramental expression of the initiation process. Therefore, "Educational aspects are secondary because confirmation is neither tied to adolescence nor a rite of passage or maturity."[38] Martinez's warnings about the primacy of the educational lend theological support to catechists' laments of losing contact with young people after confirmation. If confirmation becomes a reward or a moment of choice at the end of a program of catechesis, it loses its identity.

Confirmation's connection with baptism seems to preclude it from taking on the role of a "choice" or "commitment" ceremony. Paul Turner argues along these lines:

> Asking for commitment raises . . . problems: Is it too early to ask a teen for a commitment? Or too late? Do we presume that baptized children have no commitment to the church prior to teenage confirmation? If so, why are they coming to communion? And hasn't experience over the last 20 years shown us that teens fed up with the church frequently give a different spin on confirmation? It's not a commitment sacrament, it's a goodbye sacrament.
>
> If commitment to the church is best made when one has reached a certain age of maturity, the wisdom of baptizing infants comes quickly into question.
>
> Evaluating and committing to a cause is a human phenomenon that occurs over and over within a person's life. If confirmation fits with commitment it will need to be repeatable. Otherwise we are raising a generation of soon-to-be-disillusioned adolescents who thought the commitment they once made would stick for a lifetime.[39]

Undergirding Turner's argument is both his historical study of confirmation and his extensive pastoral experience.[40] Turner argues that functionally, confirmation celebrated as commitment serves as a time that young people see themselves as finished with activity in the church, but he also stands among several who begin to see the challenge such an approach brings to the practice of infant baptism.

Martinez and Turner represent a shift in thinking about confirmation and its pastoral applications; a shift which is duly reflected in looking at Mahony's, Levada's, and the USCCB's statements on confirmation throughout this period. The American church, in general, is becoming less optimistic about young people making a choice for Catholicism at confirmation.

"Restoring the Order"

In 1997 Bishop Joseph Gerry of Portland, Maine wrote a pastoral letter highlighting the correspondence of the canonical age for confirmation with that of First Eucharist and calling his diocese to integrate confirmation preparation into the religious education curriculum for second graders so that they may receive confirmation immediately preceding First Communion.[41] In the years that followed, Portland became an unofficial center of what would come to be called the movement to "restore the order" of the sacraments of initiation, the most organized response to the now pervasive theology of commitment articulated in terms of "choice."[42]

The groundwork for Portland's move, however, had been laid in the years preceding. As the theology of confirmation as adult choice had begun to be widely implemented, pastoral experience illustrated its problems and theologians, too, became more critical of it. The shift in John Roberto's thought is illustrative in this regard. Roberto's 1978 analysis of confirmation in the United States argued that the conflation of Thomistic theology with psychological advances resulted in a confusing amalgam which was most prevalent across U.S. dioceses. In that study, Roberto cited the importance of celebrating the sacraments in the order of baptism-confirmation-Eucharist, but did not think it was possible to restore it for the young. Based on John Westerhoff's model of faith development, he implored, "We must give young people the freedom of choice as to when they wish to celebrate the sacrament. This means that confirmation cannot be locked into one age group or grade level, rather young people will choose to celebrate the sacrament (with the help of their parents and the parish's pastoral staff) based upon their spiritual readiness."[43] In 1992 Roberto points to a new trend: "The Roman Catholic Church has an initiation theology and practice that point the way out of the present chaos by restoring the integrity of the sequence, baptism-confirmation-eucharist." Roberto offers the "restored order" as an alternative to high school confirmation. He finds the latter underdeveloped and often "a rite of graduation and, in many cases, an exit from the Catholic Church."[44] Judging by diocesan analyses and catechetical materials, Roberto's diagnosis of high school confirmation is accurate.

This "restore the order" movement approaches the formation problem in a different way. Instead of responding to the culture-wide emphasis on choice by designating confirmation as the time of choice, those who want to "restore the order" appeal to various theological precedents in order to combat the "graduation syndrome" that has developed in celebrating confirmation. They argue that confirmation has its proper place before Holy Eucharist in the order of initiation, and that it is, therefore, not the proper end of Christian initiation.

Such an argument is, of course, based on a particular reading of the history of the sacraments in question. Among sacramental theologians and liturgists, the debate centered on the relationship between baptism and confirmation and the implications for the theology of confirmation that follow. Those calling for a restored order largely think of Catholic practice immediately before *Quam Singulari* (1910) as normative. Taking into account the long history of the church allows for some variety in historical arguments.

Aidan Kavanagh's 1988 book *Confirmation: Origins and Reform,* did much of the historical and liturgical work necessary to fuel the reaction to the gradual postponement of confirmation. It was Kavanagh who John Roberto had in mind as the exemplar of his "Liturgical/Initiation School." Kavanagh focuses the beginning of this work on the *Apostolic Tradition* (ca. AD 215–20) which contains the earliest version of a confirmation prayer, thought by most scholars to be an invocation of the Holy Spirit. Kavanagh discovers that this "confirmation prayer" in the baptismal rite was not an invocation of the Holy Spirit, but rather part of the rite's dismissal. He argues that "the result [of this discovery] is to shift the emphasis on the giving of the Holy Spirit away from what would later be called 'consignation' and 'confirmation' toward baptism itself and the eucharist."[45] This shift informs Kavanagh's assertion that confirmation should remain firmly in between baptism and First Eucharist and that this order, in whatever form, is the most important aspect of the discussion.[46] Kavanagh sees the whole of confirmation reform following the council as moving toward this order.[47]

Considering RCIA as a model for Christian initiation means, for Kavanaugh, that its order of baptism-confirmation-Eucharist must be upheld. Kavanagh argues that the matter has trinitarian import: "To confirm anyone at whatever age apart from the closest possible reference to baptism, or to make a practice of confirming only well after the eucharist has begun to be received, is to render less than necessary the relationship between the missions of the Son and the Spirit, to occlude the way in which Son and Spirit come with the Father upon the baptized, and to sunder the paschal mystery."[48] Rupturing this trinitarian form should not be taken lightly, argues Kavanagh, for the order bespeaks what it celebrates.

While Kavanagh provides evidence for celebrating confirmation in between baptism and First Eucharist, he does not do so in reaction to ritualizing the adult (and, therefore presumably permanent) choice for Catholicism. Kavanagh had argued in his earlier work that adult baptism was normative in the early church and should therefore be so in the contemporary church.[49] For him, the question about commitment was solved by sidelining the messiness of infant baptism, "a benign ab-normality."[50] Confirmation need not be a rite of commitment or choice because baptism should be.

Joseph Martos challenges whether the "restored order" is really more faithful to early church practice, arguing that "when examined closely, the early history of confirmation does not strongly support a practice of being confirmed before first Communion." He argues that "the 'original sequence' to which the liturgists point is not found in any church documents before the third century." At this time, Martos suggests, the standard was baptism followed by a first participation in the Eucharistic meal. Yet, "at various places around the Roman Empire the rite of baptism often (but not always) included an anointing with oil before and/or after the immersion and/or laying-on of hands by the bishop. This anointing . . . was not a separate rite and it did not have a meaning separate from baptism."[51] Where Kavanagh emphasizes this anointing as key to understanding confirmation theology, Martos sees in it no relevant connection to confirmation, "Liturgical theologians sometimes use these historical facts to argue that the meaning of confirmation is not really different from the meaning of baptism. But the same facts could be used to argue that at this point in history, confirmation as a separate sacramental rite simply did not exist. Therefore, it cannot be said that baptism *and confirmation* must precede first Eucharist."[52] Martos clearly has Kavanagh's work in mind here.

Martos's narrative continues through the fourth century, when there is agreement about the development of confirmation as a distinct rite from baptism. In the West, he argues, when catechumens became so numerous that bishops could not be present at all local baptisms, "candidates were baptized and they attended their first eucharistic liturgy in their local parish. Later they either went to the cathedral to be anointed by the bishop or they waited until he came to confirm their baptism formally." During the first centuries, Martos continues, initiation was a process normally undertaken by adults, not children. A comparison, then, between early adult baptism and current infant baptism rests "on very shaky historical grounds."[53] Martos argues that when confirmation became a rite of its own, it was most often celebrated in the West *after* Eucharist, since the newly baptized immediately took their place at the eucharistic table. Since with baptism, children are members of the church who can receive Eucharist and the sacrament of marriage, he sees no need to insist on confirmation for full initiation. Instead, Martos poses a radical solution: confirmation should only be received by those who will take active ministry in the church. Confirmation as "ecclesial commissioning" would benefit not only the confirmand who will "feel recognized and empowered for service," but also the church community who "needs to be reminded from time to time what full, mature, committed membership in the community is all about."[54] He accuses those who push for a "restored order" to have based their arguments on either mere "liturgical legalism" or downright "liturgical magic."[55]

Like Kavanagh, Paul Turner provides some strong historical arguments for closely uniting baptism and confirmation, as the latter is the logical completion of the former. However, unlike Kavanagh and Martos, Turner finds historical reasons for concluding that baptizing children was likely an early practice of the church. Turner suggests that *"The New Testament neither proves nor excludes the possibility that infants were baptized, but it is reasonable to assume that they were."*[56] This openness is paired with the same openness to children's place at the eucharistic table at the same time. Turner employs a hermeneutic of reasonable possibility to the indemonstrable historical circumstances around children's sacramental participation. He is, therefore, more favorably disposed to infants' reception of both baptism and Eucharist in the contemporary context. In the second and third centuries Turner finds clear evidence that infant baptism and infant communion were practiced although not unanimously agreed upon. Reading the *Apostolic Tradition*, he emphasizes that the newly baptized receive Eucharist as part of the baptismal celebration.[57]

Turner agrees with Martos that when confirmation or chrismation arose as a separate rite, the baptized continued to be admitted to the eucharistic table before their baptism was confirmed by the bishop.[58] This runs as a theme in Turner's story through the tenth century: any time that confirmation was deferred, Eucharist never was. After the tenth century, the practice of the newly baptized communicating died out rather quickly and was ultimately forbidden by Leo X (1513–21).[59] Throughout Turner's narrative, the sequence of the sacraments remains widely in flux.[60] For this reason, veritably all positions find some grounding in history so "History will need the support of theology and a sensible pastoral practice." Turner argues that celebrating confirmation with or before First Eucharist is helpful but does not go far enough. Baptism, confirmation, and Eucharist celebrated universally in one rite best combines these three aspects—history, theology, and pastoral practice.[61] Turner's position represents a variant of the "restore the order" argument, which finds no particular "order" so strongly embedded in Christian history that it could be restored. Nevertheless, he finds the baptism-confirmation-

Eucharist order most compelling and especially pastoral concerns lead him to argue for a single celebration of the three in infancy.

While the diocese of Portland, Maine became the center of gravity for the movement, other dioceses had made similar moves in the years preceding Portland's, with less fanfare. Keeping in line with *Quam Singulari* and its effects on canon law, First Eucharist is still celebrated around "the age of reason" generally accepted as about seven. Often, the "restored order" places confirmation in the same liturgical celebration as First Eucharist. In one respect, these moves are attempts to do what Pius X failed to do: to account for confirmation in the context of baptism and First Eucharist.

Enrico Hernandez, whose 1997 master's thesis is an extended argument for the adoption of the "restored order," identifies Columbus, Ohio; Greensburg, Pennsylvania; Sacramento, California; Spokane, Washington; and Saginaw, Michigan among those dioceses that have developed this sacramental sequence by the time of his writing.

After Hernandez's study, other dioceses made similar moves including Fargo, North Dakota (2002), Marquette and Gaylord, Michigan (2003), Phoenix, Arizona (2005), and Tyler, Texas (2005) among them.[62] In addition many have "restored the order" at the parish level.[63] Hernandez cites its consonance with historical practice (including *Quam Singulari*) and the 1983 Code of Canon Law as his major reasons for adopting the "restored order."[64] Recalling RCIA as paradigmatic for Christian Initiation, Hernandez could have also cited, as did Kavanagh, the order of the sacraments in RCIA as an argument for his position.

Monsignor Michael Henchal cites similar historical reasons for "restoring the order," although he does not mention *Quam Singulari*. Henchal adds two significant points about the order of celebration. First, he mentions the ecumenical implications, "The churches of the East have maintained from the very beginning the practice of confirming infants at the time of baptism." Second, he points out the pastoral failure of the adolescent approach, "an emphasis on personal commitment has exactly the opposite effect from what is intended"; it provides a time for a choice away from the sacrament and out of the church that the adolescent would not normally make.[65] The latter is particularly noteworthy because of the claims to pastoral effectiveness of the adolescent commitment approach emphasized in its development.

During especially the latter part of this final period of the twentieth century many of those involved in "restoring the order" are dissatisfied with the pastoral and theological results of celebrating confirmation as a time of commitment or choice. This chapter has illustrated that the theology of confirmation that emphasizes personal choice is a development heavily influenced by a hefty cultural emphasis on choice. As such, its results are disappointing for catechists and pastoral ministers who are interested in the ongoing formation of young people and adults in the church. The push to "restore the order" of the sacraments of initiation arises later in this period as an organized example of dissatisfaction with the theologies of confirmation that emphasize the individual choice of the confirmand. However, relatively few dioceses throughout the United States adopted the "restored order" and several that had adopted it in the early nineties eventually returned to celebrating confirmation after First Eucharist. Statements from Pope Benedict XVI gestured toward its reinvigoration.[66] Celebrating confirmation before First Eucharist is a clear acknowledgement of the failures of confirmation as the time for an adolescent's choice. In the long-run, it may well be an effective *lex orandi, lex credendi* solution. In the short-run, dioceses in the United States currently celebrate confirmation at a variety of times on a variety of occasions.

Bishop Samuel Aquila of Fargo, North Dakota (now Archbishop of Denver, Colorado) reported that during his *ad limina* visit with Pope Benedict XVI on March 8, 2012, the latter approved and congratulated him on moving confirmation before First Eucharist and asked if he had begun to speak to other bishops about doing the same.[67]

Chapter 5

A Way Forward for Confirmation?

The sacraments are the proclamation of the Church: they show the world what the Church is and what it is called to become; they challenge the Church at the very moment they affirm it.

Louis-Marie Chauvet, *Symbol and Sacrament*[1]

Pneumatology should . . . describe the impact, in the context of a vision of the Church, of the fact that the Spirit distributes his gifts as he wills and in this way builds up the Church.

Yves Congar, *I Believe in the Holy Spirit*[2]

Throughout the twentieth century, confirmation has been fluidly adapted to the shifting relationship between Catholics and the wider U.S. culture. In the final period, the individualism that had been bubbling under the surface of confirmation comes to the fore in hyper form—isolating confirmation as a time of choice—with deleterious effects. Various responses to the pastoral effects of celebrating confirmation as the particular sacrament of Christian choice have arisen. At this point, it is fair to ask how to move forward.

A pastoral and theological response to confirmation in our current context must begin pneumatologically. After all, a particular connection to the Holy Spirit has been consistent throughout confirmation's variegated history. Following the Second Vatican Council, the rite of confirmation was revised in a way—informed by *ressourcement* theology—that made the Person of the Holy Spirit more central to its celebration. The Catholic charismatic renewal's appropriation of confirmation saw particularly clearly the connection between the Holy Spirit and confirmation, emphasizing—sometimes narrowly—the gifts of Spirit, especially the extraordinary ones (see chapter 3). Confirmation understood as the moment of choice, too, has its roots in a particular understanding of the Spirit's work: the Spirit who frees and the Spirit who inspires Christian apostolic action. That the problems confirmation is facing are pneumatological problems is perhaps made even more evident by the ecclesiological difficulties it raises.

Unpacking the problem of confirmation lays bare a deeper conflict about the church as U.S. Catholics face it. A Catholic ecclesiology is very difficult to maintain when voluntaristic influences dominate the American cultural landscape, almost disabling those in the United States from imagining the church as anything but "a voluntary association of men," to use John Locke's famous phrase. The individualizing tendencies of early confirmation theologies—that one is given certain gifts to be a soldier for Christ and sent on one's way, so to speak—were always buffered by the Catholic subculture that convinced young Catholics in their day-to-day lives that this best made sense in the wider context of the Catholic community. As we reach the final period, confirmation bears the full weight of American individualism and voluntarism, which suggests that one's identity is found through a mature, individual choice, rather than negotiated in the context of a long inheritance.[3] The problem in transferring this idea of identity to Catholicism is that it cannot hold the delicate interplay of person and tradition characteristic of identity in the church. Put lucidly by theologian Kimberly Hope Belcher, "the structures of Christian identity are not bounded by autonomous individuality, but neither are they compatible with complete and utter dependency."[4] Any approach to confirmation needs to embrace this apparent paradox. If the difficulty at the heart of the confusion over confirmation is ecclesiological, it is also by association pneumatological. After all, Christ's gift of the Spirit brought the church into existence at Pentecost. It is the Spirit that gives birth to Christian identity. The third article of the Apostles' Creed begins, "I believe in the Holy Spirit" and moves immediately to the "the Holy Catholic Church." On one level, reflections on the Spirit are reflections on the church and vice versa. When these two—Spirit and church—are pulled apart to any great extent, difficulties result, usually ones that pertain to the role of the individual.

That individualism is a problem for ecclesial formation is not shocking. If the argument pursued throughout this book—Catholics' changing

relationship to the wider U.S. culture heavily impacts confirmation theology and practice—is correct, then it is clearer why the struggles to form
young Catholics in the church brought about by this changing cultural
relationship are often associated with confirmation. The relationship is
mutually informing. *Quam Singulari* opened the possibility of inserting
confirmation into the tenuous teenage years and popular psychology
encouraged the same. With a theology that was far from crystal clear to
start, confirmation became a suitable beast of burden for various post-
subcultural solutions to the problem of making young Catholics adult
Catholics.

Conscious of confirmation's many faces throughout the past hundred
years, my objective has not been to develop a new theology of confirmation. Rather it has been to tell the story of confirmation theology and
practice in the United States in a way that highlights generally underemphasized aspects of the conversation—cultural shifts, individualism,
and voluntarism—in order to help pinpoint the especially pastoral difficulties experienced with the sacrament, while enriching the theological
and historical context of the confirmation question in the United States.
Accordingly, in this final chapter, I offer some brief pneumatological
reflections in view of the ongoing conversation about confirmation and
ecclesial formation. These reflections will be guides pointing to several
approaches to confirmation that emphasize the sacrament's wider ecclesial context and so allow for it to be part of the larger picture of Christian
formation in the Holy Spirit. These approaches, I think, are models for
how the thinking about the confirmation question needs to proceed.

I deliberately prescind from developing my own theology of confirmation for at least three reasons. First, there are a multitude of approaches already in print and practice, many of which have real merit.
Second, developing a theology of confirmation has not been the aim
of the project as a whole. While the book may be unconventional in
that regard, it has hopefully begun to address what I perceive to be a
general lack in the conversation—a study of the relationship between
the confirmation question and Catholics' place in wider U.S. culture.
Third, as will be clear in the examples, I think there is legitimate room
for diversity among approaches to confirmation because a measure of
prudential judgment is necessary. I do, however, think the conversation
needs to be nudged in the direction of an emphasis on the Holy Spirit,
an emphasis on ecclesial formation, as well as a conscious awareness of
a certain individualism that can arise when the confirmand's response
of choice is overemphasized. These emphases are maintained in several

already articulated approaches to confirmation that assume or argue for different occasions or ages of celebration. The study has illustrated that the problem cannot be simply reduced to either one or both of those latter questions.

I must say a bit more about what I mean by an emphasis on the Holy Spirit in confirmation because such an emphasis can take myriad forms. Throughout the study we have seen various approaches to understanding the Spirit's role in confirmation. The Third Person of the Trinity is particularly important in moving forward with the confirmation discussion because of at least two particular aspects of the Spirit's presence.

First, as noted in chapter 3, the revised rite of confirmation makes the *Person* of the Holy Spirit central. "Be sealed with the gift of the Holy Spirit." The *gift* here is the Spirit. The Spirit's gifts have a place in the rite, but their role is secondary. The first impulse here might be to distinguish the effects of baptism from those of confirmation, which would lead to the protestation that the Holy Spirit has already been received in baptism. If, instead, we look to confirmation as a celebration of the *Person* of the Holy Spirit, the emphasis changes. In confirmation we celebrate an ongoing relationship with a *Person*. The church never considers anyone to have fully encompassed the Spirit, or really to have received the Spirit in the Spirit's completeness.

Such an emphasis on the Person of the Spirit does not overrule or detract from the peculiar grace of confirmation, which I believe St. Thomas Aquinas had correct. As the *Summa Theologiae* indicates, confirmation is about strengthening the Christian.[5] Notice that describing the grace as strengthening clearly indicates the role of confirmation in formation—Christian discipleship precedes and follows this sacrament. It is strengthened in confirmation.

Sometimes when we think of receiving a sacrament—this appears to be especially true in the case of confirmation—we reflexively think about receiving some*thing*. Informed by economic exchange, we perform a certain number of hours of community service or we demonstrate a certain level of knowledge or even a measure of piety and, in turn, we receive grace in the celebration of the sacrament. Unlike the world of production, in which we speak of exchanging commodities, however, in confirmation we celebrate a relationship with a God who ultimately eludes all of our attempts at commodification.[6] God's relationship with us is actualized by grace—which is the name for God's gifts that substantiate that relationship.

Louis-Marie Chauvet helps us to see grace in the wider context of the Christian life. Far too often, Chauvet explains, we have gotten caught up in thinking of grace as a "thing" that restores in our souls that which has been depleted by human sinfulness. Coming to the sacraments, then, is much like a car filling up at a gas station. This faulty understanding of grace leads to a host of problems. It instrumentalizes grace and places us before God as consumers in the market, rather than as sons and daughters of the loving Father. In this

Louis-Marie Chauvet is a contemporary French theologian who has renewed the theology of the sacraments in recent years by questioning the dominance of Thomistic approaches and integrating more recent continental philosophy, such as the philosophy of language and Martin Heidegger's critique of metaphysics.

mode, it makes sense that one would exchange a demonstration of one's maturity for the grace of the sacrament. Or choose the Catholic Church from among the various options available and, after so doing, receive the benefits—grace—that come with such a choice. Chauvet calls us to consider grace rather as "gift," outside of the logic of the market. By its very nature grace is elusive. Chauvet points to the Exodus account of the gift of manna in the desert as paradigmatic: it sustains the Israelites, but disappears when they try to hoard it; it resembles the dewfall, which evaporates quickly, but is more substantive; its very name is a question *"Man hu?"* or *"What is this?"*[7] It is no mistake that the new translation of Eucharistic Prayer II asks God to "send your Spirit upon these gifts like the dewfall." That first epiclesis, or invocation of the Holy Spirit, makes the connection between the Eucharist and the manna in the desert clear, but also indicates the connection between the Spirit's work in the sacraments and the incalculable quality of grace. Grace is God's gift that draws us more deeply into relationship with God. As such, it cannot be earned or logged on a balance sheet, but it does require of us a response as return-gift: the life of faith.

Since the rite explicitly speaks of the gift of the Holy Spirit in confirmation, it seems to follow that the sacrament particularly strengthens our relationship with the Spirit—the Animator of the Church and the Wellspring of the Christian life. We have seen throughout confirmation's history ways in which the relationship to the Spirit has been emphasized, especially in the charismatic movement. One key to moving forward on the confirmation question, however, is to allow that the Spirit is manifest in different ways. Confirmandi may not have a dramatic experience of the Spirit at confirmation and that is okay. Sometimes the Spirit works more slowly and subtly.

The implication of placing more emphasis on the personal indwelling of the Holy Spirit than on the effects of that indwelling is anthropological. The Spirit's gifts are indeed important manifestations of the Spirit's presence, as evidenced by their mention in the rite, but the shift moves us from focusing on one's "choice" per se to focusing on the person as a temple of the Holy Spirit—always animated by that Spirit since baptism. This precludes us from making confirmation the definitive moment for one's "choice." The Holy Spirit's continual indwelling dictates this person's fundamental identity. This does not mean that confirmandi should not try to practice "fortitude," for example, but rather that one is not determined by one's measure of fortitude. Likewise, it does not mean that one's choice is not important, even vital, to the Christian life. But to pin that choice narrowly on confirmation disallows room for the Spirit's work throughout the Christian life.

In terms of confirmation, the Spirit's indwelling is a more stunning and anthropologically relevant claim than the effects of that indwelling. We are not most fundamentally "consumers," nor are we most fundamentally "religious persons," nor are we most fundamentally "thinkers." We are a confirmed people, *both* temples of the Holy Spirit and, as a church, *a* Temple of the Holy Spirit. In confirmation, the church recognizes the ongoing process of deification in its members. As St. Athanasius famously said in the fourth century, "The Word of God . . . assumed humanity that we might become God."[8] The Incarnation and Christ's concomitant Gift of the Holy Spirit have made Christians adopted sons and daughters of God the Father. Further reflection upon the implications of God's adoption, especially in Eastern Christianity, has emphasized the Christian life as a gradual deepening of participation in the very life of God. Even though they have received the Holy Spirit in baptism, Christians are recognized as temples of the Holy Spirit in confirmation, that is, as those who are becoming deified in the womb of the church. Shifting the emphasis from the will of the individual confirmand to the gift of the divine Third Person who enables all of us to partake in the divine life returns the fundamental action and initiative to God, with whom we stand in profound relationship.

Second, the Holy Spirit is One who indwells the confirmand but simultaneously, and as one Person noncontradictorily, indwells the church. The implications of the Spirit's oneness need to be central to confirmation, a celebration of the Spirit's presence in the church and, at the very same time, a celebration of the Spirit's indwelling in the person. A faulty ecclesiology bifurcates individual and church and overly separates the confirmandi, who have indeed been baptized, from the ecclesial communion. The picture is extrinsic: the confirmandi stand formally outside of the church, until they choose it, and the church performs a ritual upon them. A fuller, more deeply pneumatic ecclesiology would hold the church together. Reflecting on the significance of the practice of infant baptism, Therese Lysaught articulates the intrinsic relationship well:

> The Church reminds us that particular characteristics—like autonomy and rationality—are unimportant for what it means to be a child of God. The Church reminds us that it is not we who choose God but we who are chosen by God (Galatians 4:9). Faith is not a choice—it is a gift. Identity resides not in the ability to choose. It resides in the fact that before we are able to choose we are chosen. It reminds us that the Church is not simply one more voluntary association; it is rather a community that particularly welcomes into its midst those who are vulnerable, marginalized, those who cannot speak for themselves, those often whose ability to freely exercise their will is compromised.[9]

Emphasizing confirmation as the moment of individual choice undercuts the intimate connection between baptism and confirmation and, for the many who have been baptized as infants, performatively suggests that infant baptism is not fully efficacious, that somehow it must be ratified by individual consent. The challenge is to maintain the emphasis on faith as a gift through the sacramental sequence.

The Spirit who grants us the ability to act, to choose, to commit, does so in the context of the wider sacrament of the church. The seal is the sacramental admission of the church, in which the Spirit dwells, that recognizes the Spirit in this particular member too. The confirmandi are strengthened in that sacramental act and continue on the path of discipleship, with more and sometimes less gusto. There is the possibility that the confirmandi may drift away from the faith, but confirmation will no longer be designated as the moment when they are presented with a prime opportunity to do so.

Recall Ray Noll's reflection on the image of the church as mother cited in chapter 4—Noll claims that the church's sacramental life forms us in symbol and language in the manner a mother forms children. The gift of the Spirit made possible by the Son makes us children of the Father and sacramentally children of the church. The presence of the same Spirit in person and church is analogous to the shared presence of flesh, blood, and genes between mother and children. Pneumatologically and ecclesiologically we can see more clearly why an exaggerated emphasis on choice is incompatible with this ongoing relationship. As mentioned above, a mother does not normally provide for an appointed time at which the child must reject or accept her. If a child rejects his parents, it happens painfully and often sadly, but not on a prescribed occasion. Likewise, deeming confirmation the particular occasion for a young person's choice for (or against) the church is at odds with the fundamental relationship of person and church.

Life in Christ is not contingent upon autonomy, but is characterized by freedom. This distinction is lost on most contemporary Americans because we are so accustomed to the liberal notion of freedom, defined as choice (see the beginning of chapter 4). However, the Holy Spirit has long been identified with freedom in the Christian tradition. Here is the eminent theologian Walter Kasper on St. Paul's description of Christian life in the Spirit: "Because of the Spirit we possess the freedom of the children of God. . . . Love of God and of neighbor is true Christian freedom in the Spirit (Gal 5:13). For the free person is not the one who does whatever he wants; one who acts in that manner is very much unfree because he is the slave of himself, his moods, and his changing circumstances. The free person is rather one who is free from himself and thus able to be there for God and for others."[10] Clearly the association of freedom with confirmation—the sacrament of the Spirit—is not itself wrongheaded, for at least since St. Paul, the Holy Spirit is indeed associated with freedom. The problem lies in identifying freedom in the Spirit with the liberal notion of freedom or "choice."

The much richer, and more radical, notion of freedom in the Scriptures holds much of value in the current confirmation problematic. Christian freedom is more radical in the sense that it aims to make us free even from our own fleeting desires. Confirmation cannot, then, be reduced to an adolescent's expression or "confirmation" of the Catholic faith. Whims may change. However, the community that bears the faith of Christ, the wider context of any individual Christian's faith, remains despite those whims precisely because it, too, is anchored in Christ and enlivened by the Holy Spirit.

With these pneumatological emphases as a lens, we will now turn to several approaches articulated throughout this period that offer fruitful directions in confirmation theology and practice. In response to the twin problems of individualism and voluntarism, I do not intend to proscribe or prescribe a particular age or even time for confirmation; such questions have been pursued ad nauseam. In general, it is important for local churches to establish a uniform time for confirmation and such a decision should be made according to how the ecclesial and pneumatological aspects can best be emphasized in the particular diocese. Accordingly, the following six accounts—of four theologians and two religious educators—do not necessarily agree on the question of when confirmation should ordinarily be celebrated. Yet, they represent a common ecclesial and pneumatological emphasis that consciously challenges, instead of unconsciously reinforces, the hyper-individualism of the current context.

Jesuit theologian Gerard Fourez explicitly defers to the ecclesial context of confirmation. He argues that confirmation should be considered less as an individual's sacramental moment and more as a celebration of the coming of Holy Spirit into the church. He finds theologies that stringently identify confirmation as the sacrament of maturity individualistic and "at the least semi-pelagian."[11] He notes the uniqueness of the developmental category "adolescence" in the Western context and ultimately prescribes the age of twelve as the appropriate age "in our culture . . . to celebrate the fact that we believe the young, like the adults, can also carry the Spirit to the entire community." His answer to individualism is an emphasis on the Spirit, who dwells in both the person and the church. He lifts the burden of "choice" from confirmation, instead looking to the broader pneumatological context of Christian initiation: "The moment of confirmation is not the moment when the Spirit is received but is the moment when we celebrate this reception; and by this celebration, that reception is made more real and effective."[12]

> **Semi-pelagianism**, developed in southern France after the condemnation of Pelagianism (see p. 56 above), emphasizes a cooperative effort between God and humans in salvation, with humans taking the first step in faith. It was condemned as a heresy in 529 AD at the Council of Orange. The term itself arose much later, however, as a sixteenth-century accusation against Luis de Molina's theology of grace.

Fourez emphasizes confirmation's character as an ecclesial celebration, while not eradicating the role of the confirmand. He argues that any "sacrament, even when it is related to an individual, is always a celebration of the whole Christian community; sacraments are always celebrations of the church."[13] The church "confirms," yet the celebration is not one-sided. Since the Holy Spirit dwells in the church as in each of its members, growth and formation is mutual and ongoing. In contrast to some of those who sound individualistic notes, Fourez finds in confirmation a celebration of the entire community: "The symbolic mime of the gift of the Spirit through the Christian community (itself symbolized by the bishop) thus becomes also a celebration of a community that recognizes that the Spirit of God speaks through these new members."[14]

Aforementioned theologian German Martinez diagnoses the difficulty of individualism as extending beyond confirmation, arguing that "For many, the sacraments are individual supernatural commodities, objects of spiritual consumerism, rather than a continuing force that nurtures an experience of conversion and freedom, growth, and transformation."[15] Martinez points to the Holy Spirit as the unifying principle between church and person. He situates the encounter with the Spirit at confirmation in the narrative of the Christian people: "The communion in the Holy Spirit at confirmation re-creates the coming of God's Spirit to the world. It also communicates to the Christian community as a new Pentecost. . . . The Spirit precedes and follows confirmation."[16] Since the Holy Spirit is integral to the whole process of initiation and to confirmation and baptism in particular, Martinez argues that "It is imperative that all models [of confirmation practice] make the relationship with the Holy Spirit in the community and in the heart of the believer the fundamental referent."[17] It is from this fundamental recognition—the Holy Spirit as unifier—argues Martinez, that pedagogical and catechetical concerns should flow. The Holy Spirit's presence both in the person and the church is more fundamental to catechesis than psychology and educational theory.

Carmelite theologian Christopher O'Donnell analyzes Thomistic theology of confirmation in light of twentieth-century developments, particularly the revised Rite promulgated by Pope Paul VI in 1971. O'Donnell stresses the significance of confirmation theology for ecclesiology.[18] He reads Paul VI's revised Rite and Thomas's theology ecclesially: "it is through considering the role of the confirmed in the church that one can best explain the teaching of St. Thomas and the new rite."[19] Situating Thomas's words on confirmation ecclesially helps to avoid some of the individualistic strains that we saw during the early part of the twentieth century when theologies of confirmation depended heavily on Thomistic theology. The focus of confirmation is not the battle within the confirmand's soul, but the confirmand's role in the church.

O'Donnell also steers around the problem that John Roberto found most pressing in 1978—the combination of Thomistic theology and popular psychology, which offered widely variant understandings of maturity. St. Thomas, obviously ignorant of modern psychology, understood maturity in terms of one's place in the church, not one's fully appropriated personal faith commitment. O'Donnell's reading of the revised Rite situates it within a Thomistic framework, which counters attempts to meld the Rite with a modern individualized understanding of maturity.

Paul Turner's approach to confirmation is steeped in his extensive pastoral work as a priest. His theology is therefore firmly grounded in parish life.[20] His extensive historical work keeps him from a type of "tradition-forgetfulness," which is, in his opinion, characteristic of too many pastoral theologians. In reaction to the misuse of pastoral claims, he writes, "Pastoral theology encompasses much more than attention to the hapless predicaments of adolescents. It also commands responsible governance of symbols."[21] He sums up his bottom-line position: "The most comprehensive resolution to the issues surrounding initiation is for the West to restore full initiation at one ceremony to all candidates, regardless of age, including infants."[22] Turner argues that such a rite is the only way for Christians to maintain confirmation as clearly an initiatory sacrament.

Turner's approach is undergirded by a thick pneumatology evident in his exegetical work on the prayer of confirmation. In examining the prayer, Turner finds the Spirit's dwelling in the person and in the church connected through Christ. He acknowledges the clear invocation of the "gift" of the Holy Spirit in order to "strengthen" the candidate. He writes that *the* gift of the Holy Spirit is traditionally manifested through particular gifts. Drawing on Isaiah 11:1–3, which describes the gifts of the Spirit to be bestowed on the ruler from the line of Jesse, he connects the prayer inextricably with the salvific mission of Christ for all of humanity and with the Spirit's role in that salvation. Through liturgical usage, the prayer is personalized and as such, "masterfully weaves the role of the Holy Spirit in universal salvation with the Spirit's role in the individual Christian life."[23] Turner's exegesis of the prayer is itself masterful. He connects the liturgical prayer of the church with the personal indwelling of the Spirit, acknowledging Christ, the bearer of universal salvation, as the linchpin—"the Spirit which filled Christ will now fill those to be confirmed."[24]

Among religious educators, too, there are approaches that emphasize confirmation's ecclesial center and therefore prove fruitful in an individualistic context. Many, indeed most, of those who teach religious education

> **The Prayer of Confirmation**
> All-powerful God, Father of our Lord Jesus Christ,
> by water and the Holy Spirit you freed your sons and daughters from sin
> and gave them new life.
> Send your Holy Spirit upon them
> to be their Helper and Guide.
> Give them the spirit of wisdom and understanding,
> the spirit of right judgment and courage,
> the spirit of knowledge and reverence.
> Fill them with the spirit of wonder and awe in your presence.
> We ask this through Christ our Lord.
> Amen.
> (*Rite of Confirmation*, 25)

> "But a shoot shall sprout from
> the stump of Jesse,
> and from his roots a bud
> shall blossom.
> The spirit of the LORD shall
> rest upon him:
> a spirit of wisdom and of
> understanding,
> A spirit of counsel and of
> strength,
> a spirit of knowledge and
> of fear of the LORD,
> and his delight shall be the
> fear of the LORD"
> (Isaiah 11:1–3)

at the parish level do not call teaching their primary vocation. Ted Furlow is a general contractor who prepares young people for confirmation. His article is more of an educational success story than a programmatic approach to confirmation, but his attention to the formative aspects of life in the church is notable. His parish in Long Beach, California confirms teenagers. Furlow was thrust into preparing these teenagers for confirmation in an emergency situation; he even compares it to being thrown into deep water by his father at age six when he was unable to swim. Furlow describes the jaded responses of fellow catechists who continually lamented the disappearance of young people after confirmation—"the prophecy becomes self-fulfilling as we see them walking out the door. And instead of changing what we are doing, our response is, 'See, I told you so!'"[25] Instead of adding to this din, Furlow explores what the church can learn from younger Catholics, in a word, he tries to see the Spirit's work in them, in their seemingly odd ways of communicating, in their struggles and off-putting remarks. He writes, "If I wish to teach or communicate the 'good news' to them, then I must be able to recognize and adjust to the very unique 'who' and 'what' they are and adapt to their rhythm."[26]

While Furlow's piece has neither the precision nor nuance of an academic analysis, it gets at the heart of the difficulty—that of a sharp cultural difference between teachers and students—and addresses it head-on. Since confirmation has changed to reflect the different relationship between Catholics and U.S. culture, adults are too often caught drawing exclusively and uncontextually on their own reception of confirmation (or what they wished it would have been) in educating young Catholics. Furlow avoids this trap. It is significant that in discussing confirmation, he discusses the formative process of young Catholics and does not place the pressure of this formation on the shoulders of confirmation. Instead of offering them a time to choose, he offers them the life of a church that helps to bear life's burdens and to carry one's cross before, during, and beyond the sacrament of confirmation. He writes, "We did not give our students a two-year course of religious education; we taught them a lifetime, experiential catechesis of faith, a walk through life with the God who loves them and the certainty that they are never alone."[27] He makes the Spirit present to them via his role in the church—that Spirit who impels us toward continual death to self. Confirmation, then, is neither a beginning nor an end. It is a celebration of a relationship with that Spirit who is alive in each person and the church as a whole.

Joan Eckstein, another educator, situates confirmation within the overall context of ecclesial formation in the Spirit. In RCIA the three initiation sacraments are celebrated together after a lengthy catechumenate, which, she argues, alleviates some of the formation concerns among those baptized as adults. Among those baptized as infants, however, the formative nature of the sacraments of initiation is paramount. Therefore, she argues, confirmation is ill-considered if theologized apart from infant baptism. In the light of infant baptism, "Our Christian commitment is the response to God's initiative. It is for those who discover and accept the invitation and gift of God and allow the gift to transform them into the creatures they are thereby capable of becoming for His glory."[28]

Eckstein conducted a survey of parishes in the Archdiocese of Cincinnati in 1986 and found that the majority of parishes continued to celebrate confirmation in the junior high school years. While she acknowledges that there are other trends in different dioceses, she encourages the strengthening of postconfirmation education programs.[29] At the center of her concerns is a strong affirmation of ecclesial formation: "The goal of Christian initiation is the formation of a spirit-filled community of deeply committed Christian adults who bear witness to a faith in Christ and glorify their Father. The process of formation is a recurring theme. Thus a program for the sacraments can never divorce itself from the process of formation."[30] Eckstein was so convinced by her historical study of the intimate connection between baptism and confirmation that she "would personally recommend celebrating confirmation at baptism and developing a repeatable liturgy which could be celebrated at moments of increased personal commitment."[31] This concern too is centered on, and attempts to account for, the formation of young Catholics into adult Catholic life.

These theologians and educators have paved a road to follow for the future of confirmation celebration. As we ponder confirmation's many faces throughout the twentieth century in the United States, searching for clearer ways to communicate to young Catholics that they have been chosen by God, may we proceed with an emphasis on the Holy Spirit burning in our hearts thanks to Christ's gift of his same Spirit to the church.

Notes

Introduction

1. See Debra Campbell, "The Heyday of Catholic Action and the Lay Apostolate, 1929–1959," in *Transforming Parish Ministry: The Changing Roles of Catholic Clergy, Laity, and Women Religious*, ed. Jay P. Dolan (New York: Crossroad, 1990), 222–52.

2. William L. Portier, "Here Come the Evangelical Catholics," *Communio* 31 (Spring 2004): 45–46.

3. Louis-Marie Chauvet, *Symbol and Sacrament: A Sacramental Reinterpretation of Christian Existence*, trans. Patrick Madigan and Madeleine Beaumont (Collegeville, MN: Liturgical Press, 1995), 363.

Chapter 1
Confirmation, the Liturgical Movement, and Catholic Action: 1910–1959

1. Sacred Congregation of the Discipline of the Sacraments, *Quam Singulari: Decree on First Communion* (August 8, 1910), canon 1, http://www.papalencyclicals.net/Pius10 /p10quam.htm (accessed February 7, 2005).

2. Joseph Martos, *Doors to the Sacred: A Historical Introduction to Sacraments in the Roman Catholic Church*, rev. and updated ed. (Liguori, MO: Triumph, 2001, orig. pub. 1981), 259. Paul Turner also discusses the shift in *Confirmation: The Baby in Solomon's Court, Revised and Updated* (Chicago: Hillenbrand Books, 2006), 98–99. See also Linda Gaupin, "Now Confirmation Needs Its Own *Quam Singulari*," in *When Should We Confirm? The Order of Initiation* (Chicago: Liturgy Training Publications, 1989), 85–93, which discusses the impact of the decree and places the origins of teenage reception of the Eucharist in the seventeenth century.

3. Pius X, *Acerbo Nimis: On Teaching Christian Doctrine* (April 15, 1905), no. 22, http://www.vatican.va/holy_father/ pius_x/encyclicals/documents/hf_p-x_enc _15041905 _acerbo-nimis_en.html (accessed February 1, 2006).

4. Steven M. Avella with Jeffrey Zalar, "Sanctity in the Era of Catholic Action: The Case of St. Pius X," *U.S. Catholic Historian* 15 (Fall 1997): 74–76. Avella and Zalar

describe the development of the cult of Pius X in the United States; his interactions with children play a large role in his veneration.

5. Ibid., 75. Avella and Zalar cite as an example the diocese of Detroit in which bishop and priests were notably unenthusiastic about the shift.

6. Ibid., 75–77. Avella and Zalar discuss the change in the images on First Communion certificates—from Old Testament typologies of the Eucharist (such as Melchizedek and the sacrifice of Isaac) to portraits of Pius X.

7. Cf. Turner, *Confirmation*, 98–99, and Martos, *Doors to the Sacred*, 200.

8. By "Catholic Revival," I mean "the creating, defending, and spreading of a vibrant Catholic culture in the United States—making Catholicism a way of life." This is Anne Klejment's definition from " 'Catholic Digest' and the Catholic Revival, 1936–1945," *U.S. Catholic Historian* 21, no. 3 (Summer 2003): 94–95.

9. Debra Campbell, "The Heyday of Catholic Action and the Lay Apostolate, 1929–1959," in *Transforming Parish Ministry: The Changing Roles of Catholic Clergy, Laity, and Women Religious*, ed. Jay P. Dolan (New York: Crossroad, 1989), 225.

10. Ibid., 223. Campbell notes the liturgical movement's emphasis on lay participation in the Eucharist and its flourishing at European abbeys.

11. Ibid., 226. Campbell also notes here that the audience shaped both the tone and subject matter of the journal.

12. Basil Stegmann, "Confirmation, the Armor of the Soul," *Orate Fratres* 2 (March 1928): 135. Stegmann points to the practice of the early church here in which confirmation was celebrated "in connection with, or soon after, Baptism" to support his position.

13. Virgil Michel, "Confirmation: Our Apathy," *Orate Fratres* 2 (April 1928): 167–71; Michel, "Confirmation: Its Divine Powers," *Orate Fratres* 2 (May 1928): 199–204; and Michel, "Confirmation: Call to Battle," *Orate Fratres* 2 (June 1928): 234–39.

14. Michel, "Confirmation: Our Apathy," 170.

15. For a pastoral example of the imagery and of catechetical method during the period, see M. Chrysantha, "Becoming Soldiers of Jesus Christ: A Unit for the Upper Grades," *Journal of Religious Education* 2 (May 1932): 810–29.

16. Ibid., 169.

17. Cf. John Lancaster Spalding, *The Baltimore Catechism No. 3* (New York: Benziger Brothers, 1885), question 673, and Francis J. Connell, *The New Confraternity Edition of the Revised Baltimore Catechism No. 3* (New York: Benziger Brothers, 1949), question 330.

18. Michel, "Confirmation: Its Divine Powers," 199–200. See Thomas Aquinas, *Summa Theologica*, trans. Fathers of the English Dominican Province (New York: Benziger Brothers, 1947), III.72.11, rep. obj. 2.

19. Michel, "Confirmation: Its Divine Powers," 201.

20. Michel, "Confirmation: Its Divine Powers," 200, 203 (emphasis in original).

21. Keith F. Pecklers, *The Unread Vision, The Liturgical Movement in the United States of America: 1926–1955* (Collegeville, MN: Liturgical Press, 1998), 128–29.

22. Michel, "Confirmation: Call to Battle," 238 (emphasis in original).

23. Campbell, "The Heyday of Catholic Action," 223.

24. Quoted in William T. Cavanaugh, *Torture and Eucharist: Theology, Politics, and the Body of Christ*, Challenges in Contemporary Theology, ed. Gareth Jones and Lewis

Ayers (Malden, MA: Blackwell, 1998), 137. See Pius XI, *Quadragesimo Anno*, 88, 109, in David J. O'Brien and Thomas A. Shannon, *Catholic Social Thought: The Documentary Heritage* (Maryknoll, NY: Orbis, 1992), 62, 65.

25. Paul Turner, *Ages of Initiation: The First Two Christian Millennia with CD-ROM of Source Excerpts* (Collegeville, MN: Liturgical Press, 2000), CD-ROM chap. 12, sec. 6. See also, A. Bentley, "Sacrament of Confirmation: New Decisions and Decrees," *Clergy Review* 10 (1935): 63–65.

26. On this difficulty, see "Confirmation before First Communion" (letter to the editor and response), *The Ecclesiastical Review* 98 (February 1938): 160–64.

27. H. A. Reinhold, "Christian Responsibility," *Orate Fratres* 16 (October 1942): 514. See also Reinhold, "The Sacrament of Responsibility," *Commonweal* 32 (May 1940): 58–59.

28. Campbell, "The Heyday of Catholic Action," 223–24.

29. Ibid. All quotations from *Il Fermo Proposito* are from Campbell's text.

30. Theodore Hesburgh, "The Relation of the Sacramental Characters of Baptism and Confirmation to the Lay Apostolate" (Ph.D. diss., The Catholic University of America, 1946), 12, 16.

31. Pius XI, *Ex Officiosis Litteris*: Apostolic Letter to Cardinal Cerejeira Concerning Catholic Action in Portugal, *Acta Apostolicae Sedis* 25 (1934): 629.

32. Gerard Meath, "Sacerdotal Aspects of the Lay Apostolate," *Orate Fratres* 15 (September 1941): 457–63 (originally published in *New Blackfriars* 19, no. 222 [September 1938]: 668–75). Meath was Prior Provincial of the English Dominicans, 1962–1966.

33. Ibid., 457. See also Hesburgh, "The Relation of the Sacramental Characters of Baptism and Confirmation to the Lay Apostolate," 182. Drawing on Thomas Aquinas, Hesburgh describes confirmation as "midway between the characters of baptism [primarily passive and ordained for one's individual good] and holy orders [primarily active and ordained for the sanctification of others]." The character of confirmation, then, is both passive (spiritual protection) and active (apostolic and oriented toward others), yet Hesburgh is clear that the participation in Christ's priestly *munus* through confirmation is significantly less in degree than holy orders.

34. Meath, "Sacerdotal Aspects of the Lay Apostolate," 462.

35. Damasus Winzen, "Anointed with the Spirit (II): The Fruits of Confirmation," *Orate Fratres* 20 (July 1946): 393. This is the second part of Winzen's "Anointed with the Spirit," *Orate Fratres* 20 (June 1946): 337–43. Notably, Winzen writes shortly before the landmark Vatican decree that named priests extraordinary ministers of confirmation in situations where death is imminent. See "Decisions of the Holy See," *Review for Religious* 6 (January 1947): 24–27. This decree was a necessary step on the way to the revised Rite of Christian Initiation launched in 1974 at the behest of the Second Vatican Council.

36. Winzen, "Anointed with the Spirit (II)," 396.

37. Ibid., 390. See Thomas Aquinas, *Summa Theologica* III.72.4, rep. obj. 3.

38. Winzen, "Anointed with the Spirit (II), 389, n. 1.

39. Winzen, "Anointed with the Spirit," 339.

40. Ibid., 341.

41. Gregory Dix, *The Theology of Confirmation in Relation to Baptism* (Westminster: Dacre Press, 1946).

42. James R. Gillis, "The Case for Confirmation," *The Thomist* 10 (1947): 168. Gillis notes the irony and immediacy posed by the mere fact that a "case" must be articulated for the sacrament.

43. Gillis, "The Case for Confirmation," 166.

44. Ibid., 184, 182.

45. George D. Smith, "Confirmed to Bear Witness," *Worship* 26 (July 1952): 385, n. 1.

46. Ibid., 385–89.

47. Ibid., 389. Smith draws out the implications of this witness in a world where it is unpopular. He even makes the connection with accepting martyrdom if necessary, presumably drawing on the Greek root of the word martyr, "witness."

48. Ibid., 392.

Chapter 2
Confirmation and the Second Vatican Council: 1960–1971

1. For an example of this tension, see Keith F. Pecklers, *The Unread Vision, The Liturgical Movement in the United States of America: 1926–1955* (Collegeville, MN: Liturgical Press, 1998), 118–22.

2. Marcellino D'Ambrosio, "*Ressourcement* Theology, *Aggiornamento*, and the Hermeneutics of Tradition," *Communio* 18 (Winter 1991): 532. D'Ambrosio notes the double entendre of "source": the overlooked documents of the church, but also the "fountain" of tradition whose flowing waters held the source, the method, and the object of *nouvelle théologie*.

3. Joseph Martos, *Doors to the Sacred: A Historical Introduction to Sacraments in the Catholic Church*, rev. and updated ed. (Liguori, MO: Triumph, 2001, orig. pub. 1981), 110. For example, Edward Schillebeeckx found that "*ex opere operato*," the phrase used to express distance between the sacrament and its minister that had too often led to sacramental mechanism, is actually used sparingly by Thomas and serves as a building block to a much larger, nuanced sacramental theology. See Schillebeeckx's seminal work on the sacraments, *Christ the Sacrament of the Encounter with God*, trans. Paul Barrett (Franklin, WI: Sheed and Ward, 1963, orig. pub. as *Christus, Sacrament van de Godsontmoetimg* [Bilthoven: H. Nelissen, 1960]), 82–89.

4. Schillebeeckx, *Christ the Sacrament of the Encounter with God*, 200–15.

5. See Ibid., esp. 133–35. See also Karl Rahner, *The Church and the Sacraments*, Quaestiones Disputatae Series 9, trans. W. J. O'Hara (Freiburg: Herder, 1963).

6. See also Henri de Lubac's contribution to the renewal in his *Catholicism: Christ and the Common Destiny of Man*, trans. Lancelot Sheppard and Elizabeth Englund (San Francisco: Ignatius Press, 1988, French original, 1947), 82–111, where he emphasizes the role of the sacraments in upholding the unity of the church.

7. Marian Bohen, *The Mystery of Confirmation: A Theology of the Sacrament* (New York: Herder and Herder, 1963): chap. 1, esp. 7, 18–19. For examples of the Catholic Action theology of confirmation in the early sixties, see Ralph Fisher, *Confirmation: The Forgotten Sacrament* (Notre Dame: Ave Maria Press, 1961), esp. 26–28, and Sisters

Alma Marie and Helen Claire, *Preparing for Confirmation*, On Our Way Series (New York: Sadlier, 1964), the examples and stories that frame the pamphlet are shaped predominately by Catholic Action.

8. Bohen, *Mystery*, 47. For an example of a European thinker who also jettisons the "sacrament of Catholic Action" position because it does violence to the sources, see Pierre-Thomas Camelot, "La théologie de la Confirmation à la lumière des controversies recentes," *La Maison-Dieu* 54 (1958): 79–91.

9. Bohen, *Mystery*, 59–63.

10. Ibid., 184.

11. Ibid., 185–87. See also Rahner, *The Church and the Sacraments*, esp. 87–93. Rahner holds a similar position on the relationship between baptism and confirmation, describing them as degrees of one sacrament, akin to the diaconate, presbyterate, and episcopate of orders.

12. Bohen, *Mystery*, 63.

13. Ibid., 145.

14. Marian Bohen, "Confirmation Catechesis," *Worship* 38, no. 11 (January 1964): 88. The catechetical conversation is largely connected to the order of the sacraments of initiation and their identification as such. See Charles Connors, "Sacrament as Weapon?" *The Homiletic and Pastoral Review* 62, no. 5 (February 1962): 417–18, where Connors notes his impression that most U.S. dioceses delay confirmation beyond first Eucharist for catechetical reasons—so that young people continue attending religious education classes into the teenage years. Like Bohen, Connors laments the shift in emphasis from the grace of the sacrament to the knowledge gained prior to its reception.

15. Bohen's move in this regard is significant and unique not because all previous theologies of confirmation were centered on Catholic Action, but because she rejects the theology on historical grounds. At the turn of the decade there were theologians avoiding confirmation's direct association with Catholic Action apart from such patristic exegesis. For example, see J. P. Kenny, "The Age for Confirmation," *Worship* 35, no. 1 (December 1960): 14–15. Kenny argues that confirmation should be considered "the sacrament of perseverance" because the Holy Spirit comes to the individual's aid to maintain personal faith following the critical choice properly made at the age of reason.

16. *Sacrosanctum Concilium*: The Dogmatic Constitution on the Sacred Liturgy, in *Vatican Council II: Volume 1, The Conciliar and Post Conciliar Documents*: new rev. ed., ed. and trans. Austin Flannery (Northport, NY: Costello Publishing Company, 1996), no. 71.

17. Ibid., no. 64.

18. Most famously, see Aidan Kavanagh, *The Shape of Baptism* (New York: Pueblo, 1978), and Kavanagh, *Confirmation: Origins and Reform* (New York: Pueblo, 1988). Also see Robert J. Brooks, "Reflections on the Eucharist as the Continuation of Baptism," *Liturgy* 25, no. 1 (January/February 1980): 22.

19. See chapter 1, n. 33.

20. Mary Charles Bryce, "Confirmation: Being and Becoming Christian," *Worship* 41, no. 5 (May 1967): 285.

21. Ibid., 288 (emphasis added).

22. Ibid., 287.

23. Ibid, 284–85. Raymond F. Collins cites the same three commonalities in confirmation theologies in "Confirmation: A Theological Overview," *Homiletic and Pastoral Review* 70 (May 1970): 604. Like Bryce, Collins works against the gap between the celebration of baptism and confirmation.

24. Bryce, "Confirmation," 289.

25. Ibid., 291–92.

26. Ibid., 292. See also Francis Buckley, "What Age for Confirmation?" *Theological Studies* 27, no. 4 (December 1966): 656, 661. Buckley also discusses the Holy Spirit's work in confirmation in relation to the Pentecost event and Acts of the Apostles in general. He writes, "The special characteristics of this gift of the Spirit (as distinct from the prebaptismal, baptismal, and postbaptismal gifts) are visibility, power, a social purpose, and an understanding of the Christ-event to bear effective witness to others." Like Bryce, for Buckley the primary place of the Spirit's dwelling is in the hearts of Christ's followers.

27. William L. Portier, "Here Come the Evangelical Catholics," *Communio* 31 (Spring 2004): 45–46 (emphasis added).

28. Joseph Ratzinger, *The Nature and Mission of Theology: Approaches to Understanding Its Role in the Light of the Present Controversy*, trans. Adrian Walker (San Francisco: Ignatius Press, 1995), 73.

29. Buckley, "What Age for Confirmation?" 666 (emphasis added).

30. Ibid., 660. See also *Sacrosanctum Concilium*, no. 14.

31. Buckley, "What Age for Confirmation?" 659.

32. Portier, "Here Come the Evangelical Catholics," 39.

33. Joseph T. Nolan, "Rethinking Confirmation," *National Catholic Reporter* 8 (December 17, 1971): 8 (emphasis added).

34. By "contemporary psychological theory" I am thinking of its broad implications for considering the very nature of humanity, its emphasis on personal development, the development of the designation "adolescent," and its characteristic emphasis on the individual's inward search for identity. See Carl Rogers, *On Becoming a Person: A Therapist's View of Psychotherapy* (Boston: Houghton Mifflin, 1961), esp. 107–24, which discusses the process of "an individual becoming more open to his experience" (115) and in turn, "developing a trust in his own organism as an instrument of sensitive living . . . [and] accept[ing] the locus of evaluation as residing within himself" (124).

35. Jay P. Dolan, "American Catholics in a Changing Society: A Question in Search of an Answer," in *Transforming Parish Ministry: The Changing Roles of Catholic Clergy, Laity, and Women Religious*, ed. Jay P. Dolan (New York: Crossroad, 1989), 314. Dolan also links the rise in Catholic education to the general rise in education following World War II.

36. Ibid., 314–15. Dolan notes the intensification of this individualism over the next decades, when phrases such as "the me generation," "doing your own thing," and "the liberated person" characterized American culture.

37. Ibid., 315.

38. Bryce, "Confirmation: Being and Becoming Christian," 293, quoting Gordon W. Allport, *Becoming* (New Haven, CT: 1966), 96, n. 18. "Psychologically defined," writes E. M. Ligon, "religion is the integrating force of personality," *The Psychology of Christian Personality* (New York, 1961), 64.

39. See also Dorothy Watson, "Confirmation and the Adolescent," *The Furrow* 21 (April 1970): 245–46. Watson, a British sister of the Society of the Holy Child Jesus and professor of religious education, starts also with the estrangement of adolescents as her launching pad for suggestions about confirmation. She writes that for catechetical educators "a course in elementary psychology is essential to acquire a real understanding of persons"; she recommends no such course in theology. For Watson, confirmation marks responsibility, a profound stage in personal development.

40. Ibid., 298.

41. Ibid., 295.

42. Ibid., 296.

43. Ibid., 298. See also Bernard J. Cooke, Introduction to *From Baptism to the Act of Faith*, by Jean Mouroux, trans. M. Elizabeth and M. Johnice (Boston: Allyn and Bacon, 1964): vi–vii. Cooke's introduction offers a different emphasis from Bryce's; he writes, "Perhaps most important in catechetical impact has been the recent theological understanding of *faith*. Without in any way denying the essentially intellectual nature of faith, Catholic theologians are insisting more on the fact that genuine faith is a deeply personal act, a *practical* choice that involves one in the concrete life and mission of the church, a total *self-commitment* to Christ and to the achievement of his kingdom." For Cooke, it is the choice of faith that enters one into the life and mission of the church. He does not emphasize the continual remaking of this commitment. Offering a catechetical perspective, Richard Ling argues for infant confirmation, pointing to the difficulty in determining one's readiness to make a mature commitment. Ling also refers to Francis Buckley's warnings about the numerous periods of "crisis" that occur even after one's commitment. Richard Ling, "A Catechist's Vote for Infant Confirmation," *Living Light* 7 (Spring 1970): 48.

44. Collins, 607, n. 73.

45. Ibid., 608.

46. Ibid. This question of confirming those with disabilities became contested amidst the development of theologies of confirmation as maturity. See also Gerard Breitenbeck, "Should the Retarded Be Confirmed?" *Liguorian* 55 (January 1967): 26–31. Breitenbeck, who is involved in special religious education, argues against those that deny confirmation on the basis of a lack of mental ability.

Chapter 3
Confirmation and Negotiating Pluralism: 1971–1980

1. See Philip Gleason, "What Made Catholic Identity a Problem?" in *Faith and the Intellectual Life*, ed. James L. Heft (Notre Dame: University of Notre Dame Press, 1996), 87–100.

2. See, for example, John Tracy Ellis, *American Catholicism*, 2nd ed., Studies in American Religion, ed. Daniel J. Boorstin (Chicago: University of Chicago Press, 1969). The title of Ellis's fourth chapter is "Maturing Catholicism in the United States."

3. See Yves Congar, *I Believe in the Holy Spirit*, 3 vols., trans. David Smith (New York: Seabury Press, 1983), 1:167-73, where Congar elaborates the pneumatology of Vatican II, both its achievements and shortcomings.

4. "Rite of Confirmation," no. 1 in *Rites*, 479.

5. Ibid., no. 23; no. 13. For a further explication see Boniface Luykx, "On Confirmation," *Homiletic and Pastoral Review* 73 (November 1972): 61–62.

6. Apostolic Constitution on the Sacrament of Confirmation: *Divinae Consortium Naturae* (DCN), August 15, 1971, in *The Rites of the Catholic Church as Revised by the Second Vatican Ecumenical Council*, comp. National Conference of Catholic Bishops' Committee on the Liturgy, trans. International Commission for English in the Liturgy, Study Edition, Vol. 1 (Collegeville, MN: Liturgical Press, 1990), 472.

7. For example, Marian Bohen, *The Mystery of Confirmation: A Theology of the Sacrament* (New York: Herder and Herder, 1963), 184. Bohen had argued that the personal encounter with and reception of the Holy Spirit in confirmation are paramount to the effects or gifts that the Spirit gives. See chapter 2.

8. Ralph A. Keifer, "Confirmation and Christian Maturity: The Deeper Issue," *Worship* 46, no. 10 (December 1972): 608.

9. In Latin, *Accipe signaculum doni Spiritus Sancti*. For some of the challenges in rendering an adequate translation, see Robert Newton Barger, "The New Rite of Confirmation," *Worship* 45 (November 1971): 566, and also Gerard Austin, "What Has Happened to Confirmation?" *Worship* 50 (Summer 1976): 421.

10. DCN, in *The Rites*, Vol. 1, 477. Paul VI makes clear allusions to the unity of the East and the West in the anointing with chrism.

11. Luykx, "On Confirmation," 67, n. 4.

12. DCN, in *The Rites*, Vol. 1, 477. This is a particularly interesting move considering Kenan Osborne's words: "In the East and the West, over the centuries, a question on the issue of chrism and/or laying on of hands has been argued, with the West leaning toward the laying on of hands and the East leaning toward chrismation" (Kenan Osborne, *The Christian Sacraments of Initiation: Baptism, Confirmation, Eucharist* [New York: Paulist Press, 1987], 111). In this historical light, it seems even clearer that Pope Paul makes an ecumenical gesture here, causing some theological confusion.

13. DCN, in *The Rites*, Vol. 1, 477–78.

14. For some of the questions and considerations regarding the place of the laying on of hands in the rite of confirmation, see Austin, "What Has Happened to Confirmation?" 420–26. Austin critiques the pope for identifying the laying on of hands so closely with the anointing both because it flirts with the irresponsible governing of symbols (the thumb of anointing equals "hands") and because the pope's language—distinguishing what is "of the essence of the rite"—tends toward Scholastic juridicism, partitioning the rite into what is absolutely necessary and what is not. See also Barger, "The New Rite of Confirmation," 566–68.

15. Scanlan, *A Portion of My Spirit*, 1–4. For the story of the beginnings of the movement, see James Byrne, *Threshold of God's Promise: An Introduction to the Catholic Pentecostal Movement*, 3d ed. (Notre Dame: Ave Maria Press, 1971), 12–20.

16. Patrick W. Carey, *Catholics in America: A History* (Westport, CT: Praeger, 2004), 137. See also R. Scott Appleby, "The Emergence of the Orchestra Leader, 1973–," in

Transforming Parish Ministry: The Changing Roles of Catholic Clergy, Laity, and Women Religious, ed. Jay P. Dolan (New York: Crossroad, 1989), 99. Both Carey and Appleby acknowledge the centrality of the Spirit's gifts to the renewal.

17. Scanlan, *A Portion of My Spirit*, 161. "The Gallup Poll in the Fall of 1977 estimated that ten percent of the Catholics in the United States are involved in the charismatic renewal. . . . Eighty percent of those involved in the Catholic Charismatic Renewal are located in the United States."

18. Carey, *Catholics in America*, 137. Joseph Martos also notes the renewal's "unashamedly evangelical approach to Christianity and its rediscovery of New Testament forms of prayer and ritual," in *Doors to the Sacred: A Historical Introduction to Sacraments in the Catholic Church*, rev. and updated ed. (Liguori, MO: Triumph, 2001, orig. pub. 1981), 133.

19. Debra Campbell, "The Laity in the Age of Aggiornamento, 1960–1969," in *Transforming Parish Ministry: The Changing Roles of Catholic Clergy, Laity, and Women Religious*, ed. Jay P. Dolan (New York: Crossroad, 1989), 266.

20. Michael Scanlan, *A Portion of My Spirit: The Catholic Charismatic Renewal* (St. Paul, MN: Carillon Books, 1979), 89.

21. The anti-individualistic overtones did not save the renewal from critiques of individualistic spirituality, especially with regard to the workings of grace manifested in the charisms of the Spirit. These criticisms are also connected to the indeterminate relationship between the renewal and the wider Body of Christ. James F. Breckenridge, *The Theological Self-Understanding of the Catholic Charismatic Movement* (Washington, DC: University Press of America, 1980), 105–9.

22. Quoted in Scanlan, *A Portion of My Spirit*, 94.

23. See also Byrne, *Threshold of God's Promise*, who notes the tension in the church between intellectuals and charismatics. He writes, "The Charismatic Renewal is an amazing reality today. It is a powerful force which God seems to have unleashed in our midst. It is a historical and sociological phenomenon which in short time has already demonstrated its power and appeal. It is something which *even its sharpest foes—the intellectual humanists in the Church—*are being forced to face and attack" (22, emphasis added). For an example of such a thoroughly epistemological and theological critique of the charismatic renewal, see Breckenridge, *The Theological Self-Understanding of the Catholic Charismatic Movement*, esp. 6–11, 115–19. Breckenridge finds the "crisis nature" of charismatic spirituality incompatible with the "progressive nature" of mainstream Roman Catholic spirituality. Whereas Scanlan argues that "Both the growth pattern and the crisis pattern should be looked upon as authentic ways of realizing the graces of initiation at the conscious level" (*A Portion of My Spirit*, 149).

24. Cited in Scanlan, *A Portion of My Spirit*, 94.

25. Scanlan, *A Portion of My Spirit*, 62–63.

26. See Edward D. O'Connor, *The Pentecostal Movement in the Catholic Church* (Notre Dame: Ave Maria Press, 1971), esp. 221–34, who already in 1971 notes individualism as a potential danger of the movement. Another charismatic, James Byrne is an exception. In 1970–71, he writes, "The baptism in the Holy Spirit does not occur in a human void, nor is it an individual experience. It is given in the Church and for

the Church and it is generally received in the context of a local prayer community" (*Threshold of God's Promise*, 50).

27. Kevin and Dorothy Ranaghan, *Catholic Pentecostals* (New York: Paulist Press, 1969), 143.

28. O'Connor, *The Pentecostal Movement*, 136.

29. Byrne, *Threshold of God's Promise*, 49. Byrne identifies the personal nature of the baptism in the Spirit, while warding off the charge of individualism.

30. In 1969 the Ranaghans, noting the historical and theological difficulties involved with understanding confirmation, sharply distinguish between confirmation and baptism in the Spirit (*Catholic Pentecostals*, 139–40).

31. Acts 1:4-5; 2; 4:32; 8:14-18; 9; 10:44-47; 19; Eph 4; 2 Cor 1:21-22; and Luke 3:21-22 are a few examples.

32. Stephen B. Clark, *Confirmation and the Baptism of the Holy Spirit* (Pecos, NM: Dove Publications, 1969), 3. Clark was particularly struck by the theological description of confirmation's effects in the pamphlet.

33. Ibid., 5, 11, 13, 20.

34. Robert Wild, "Where There's a Will: Charismatic Renewal and a Parish Confirmation Program," *Living Light* 8 (Winter 1971): 121.

35. Ibid, 123.

36. Charles Antekeier, Van Vandagriff, and Janet Vandagriff, *Confirmation: The Power of the Spirit, A Charismatic Preparation Program for Youth, Their Parents and Sponsors*, with an introduction by Joseph C. McKinney (Notre Dame: Ave Maria Press, 1972), 10.

37. Ibid., 19, 15, 79 (emphasis in original). The authors are not alone in their identification of confirmation as a time of choice for individual young adults; such a pastoral position extends farther than that and, as we have seen, even precedes the charismatic renewal. Yet, in such a position, one can see some of the warrants for criticisms such as Breckenridge's. Similar confirmation positions will be further discussed toward the end of this chapter and throughout chapter 4.

38. Scanlan writes, "The persons involved in the renewal emphasize the necessity of personal commitment. As an adult, one cannot be Christian by proxy. One can only be a Christian by personal commitment" (*A Portion of My Spirit*, 149).

39. Glossolalia and prophecy are examples of more distinctly "charismatic" effects.

40. Antekeier, Vandagriff, and Vandagriff, *Confirmation: The Power of the Spirit*, 21, 23.

41. See, for example, Michael Delea, "Every Child's Guide to Confirmation," *Liguorian* 61 (March 1973): 44–46, and Kenneth F. Smits, "Confirmation Re-examined: An Evolving Theology and Practice," *Worship* 48, no. 1 (January 1974): 21–29.

42. Smits, "Confirmation Re-examined: An Evolving Theology and Practice," 22–23.

43. Ibid., 27.

44. Quoted in John Roberto, *Confirmation in the American Catholic Church* (Washington, DC: National Conference of Diocesan Directors of Religious Education/ CCD, 1978), 30.

45. Joseph Cunningham, "Confirmation: Pastoral Letdown," *America* 136 (February 26, 1977): 165.

46. Ibid., 165–66.

47. Ibid., 164–65.

48. LaVerne Haas, *Personal Pentecost: The Meaning of Confirmation* (Abbey Press: St. Meinrad, IN, 1973), xi.

49. Ibid., 67, 28, 13, 19.

50. Charles A. Buswell, "Pastoral Suggestions for the Celebration of Confirmation," *Worship* 46, no. 1 (January 1972): 31.

51. Buswell is by no means alone in this opinion. We saw the rise of this theology during the previous period and its role in the context of the charismatic renewal. For some noncharismatic examples not discussed in the text, see Kay Overfield, "Confirmation: Junior High Style" *Religion Teacher's Journal* 7 (January 1974): 14; John C. Tormey, "Thanks, We Needed That" *U. S. Catholic* 39 (May 1974): 17–18; Matthew Beach, "Confirmation 'Contract' Demands 'Commitment,'" *National Catholic Reporter* 12 (November 28, 1975): 3; Robert Ludwig, "Theological Appeal for Updating Confirmation," *Today's Parish* (April 1976): 14; Margot Hover, "Confirmation Marks a Passage to Maturity," *Religion Teacher's Journal* 11 (February 1978): 44. Christopher Kiesling serves as a counter example, advancing the argument that the Holy Spirit has primacy in confirmation: "The main emphasis [of confirmation] should not be shifted to our Christian commitment. Confirmation does not primarily celebrate our making a commitment, but God's gift to us of his Spirit making such a commitment possible" (*Confirmation and Full Life in the Spirit* [Cincinnati: St. Anthony Messenger Press, 1973], 159).

52. Buswell, "Pastoral Suggestions for the Celebration of Confirmation," 32. Archdiocese of Chicago associate pastor Anthony J. Brankin takes a different tact in addressing similar problems. He laments the heavy emphasis on action and personal decision in the culture, coupled with amnesia of God's saving work in the world. He offers confirmation as witness that God is working (and has worked) in the world in an actual way, to "a world already so smug and confident in its own limitless capabilities." He continues, "[Confirmation] cautions us not to put such an overwhelming emphasis on the accomplishment of tasks, the doing of projects, the meditating on self and maturity" ("Confirmation: The Mystical Seal of the Holy Spirit," *Homiletic and Pastoral Review* 80 [April 1980]: 16).

53. Buswell, "Pastoral Suggestions for the Celebration of Confirmation," 34.

54. Ibid., 32.

55. Ibid., 34.

56. Keifer, "Confirmation and Christian Maturity," 601. It seems that Keifer is referring to a gathering of mostly Evangelical Christians, but it remains unclear. Recall that Keifer found the Holy Spirit, not commitment or maturity, the clear central focus of the revised rite. Kenneth Woodward offers a similar lament regarding Christian maturity formed by the contemporary milieu: "Today . . . American Catholics—especially in the suburbs—have become so acculturated that it takes more maturity than most 13-year-olds (or their parents) can muster to recognize the many and often subtle points at which Catholics, if they are to be true to Christ, must courageously part company with their fellow Americans" (Kenneth L. Woodward, "How to Make Confirmation Signify Something," *U.S. Catholic* 41 [February 1976]: 24).

57. Ibid.

58. Ibid., 604. Woodward again echoes Keifer: the West has prolonged adolescence into an "increasingly dysfunctional period of the life cycle." In response, "the church ought to draw on the richness latent in its own sacramental tradition to restore some dignity, responsibility, and trust to early youth." Parting from Keifer, Woodward offers Mormonism as an ecclesial, familial model confident that "By rebuilding the parish on the Mormon model of the extended family, American Catholicism can capture some of the closeness and mutual concern which are the most attractive characteristics of a movement; at the same time, the fluidity and pluralism of contemporary American Catholicism should prevent the parish as I have described it from turning into a sectarian ghetto." Woodward suggests that the pluralistic influence on Catholicism is a positive deterrent to sectarianism (25).

59. Ibid., 607–9, 601.

60. Gerard P. Weber, James J. Killgallon, M. Michael O'Shaughnessy, *Growth in the Spirit: Preparation for the Celebration of Confirmation*, parent ed. (Beverly Hills: Benziger, 1974), 1, see also 59–80 passim. The authors often reiterate the impact of Catholics' wider social context on the sacrament of confirmation, 11–40 passim.

61. Ibid., 11.

62. This is the very ecclesiological problem that Portier finds endemic to Catholic life in a full-on pluralistic culture. See Portier, "Here Come the Evangelical Catholics," *Communio* 31 (Spring 2004): 43, 58.

63. John Roberto, "Confirmation in the American Catholic Church," *The Living Light* 15 (Summer 1978): 262–63. Cf. John Roberto, *Confirmation in the American Catholic Church* (Washington, DC: National Conference of Diocesan Directors of Religious Education/CCD, 1978), "Introduction." The internal quotation is to Aidan Kavanagh.

64. Cf. Roberto, *Confirmation*, 23–27. Roberto identifies some theological concerns and seven different "alterations in initiatory polity" drawn from RCIA.

65. Aidan Kavanagh, "Adult Initiation: Process and Ritual," *Liturgy* 22, no. 1 (January 1977): 8, quoted in Roberto, *Confirmation*, 33.

66. Roberto, "Confirmation," 278–79.

67. Roberto, "Confirmation," 266. Cf. Roberto, *Confirmation*, 22–23.

68. Weber, Killgallon, and O'Shaughnessy, *Growth in the Spirit*, 7 (emphasis in original). The authors quote values expert Sidney Simon, modeling the exercise around his work on values clarification. Also of note here is the preference for the more general designation "community" over "church." See also Sandy Carrubba, "Confirmation: Becoming Aware of Community," *Today's Catholic Teacher* 13 (March 1980): 20–21. Carrubba also begins with the general notion of "community" in order to understand the church.

69. Gloriani Bednarski, "A Total Parish Preparation Plan for Confirmation," *Living Light* 9 (Spring 1972): 126.

70. Bednarski, "A Total Parish Preparation Plan for Confirmation," 129. Consideration of the church and the Holy Spirit come in this program only after the participants reflect upon "What is the truth for me? What is my life meant to be?" Similarly the concurrent parent program begins with "A Psychology of Adolescence."

71. Paul Turner, *Confirmation: The Baby in Solomon's Court, Revised and Updated* (Chicago: Hillenbrand Books, 2006), 101–2.

72. Kiesling, *Confirmation and Full Life in the Spirit*, 13–14.

73. 2 Peter 1:4, quoted in Kiesling, *Confirmation and Full Life in the Spirit*, 14.

74. Ibid., 13 (emphasis added).

75. Andrew M. Greeley, "Pop Psychology and the Gospel," *Theology Today* 33, no. 3 (October 1976): 224–31.

76. Ibid., 226.

77. Ibid., 224–25. For a bit more measured, but otherwise similar, critique see Aidan Kavanagh, "Life-Cycle Events and Civil Ritual," in *Initiation Theology: Addresses of the Fourth Symposium of the Canadian Liturgical Society Held at the University of Manitoba in Winnipeg, 24–27 May 1977*, ed. James Schmeiser (Toronto: The Anglican Book Centre, 1978), 9–22.

78. Ibid., 226.

79. Quoted in William J. Freburger, "Confirmation, We Hardly Knew Ye," *The Priest* 48, no. 6 (June 1992): 28.

Chapter 4
Confirmation Theology and Practice: After 1981

1. Jay P. Dolan, "American Catholics in a Changing Society: A Question in Search of an Answer," in *Transforming Parish Ministry: The Changing Roles of Catholic Clergy, Laity, and Women Religious*, ed. Jay P. Dolan (New York: Crossroad, 1989), 306.

2. David O'Brien, "Catholic Youth: The Presumed Become the Pursued," in *The Catholic Church in the Twentieth Century: Renewing and Reimaging the City of God*, ed. John Deedy (Collegeville, MN: Liturgical Press, 2000), 97.

3. Ibid., 97–98.

4. William V. D'Antonio, James D. Davidson, Dean R. Hoge, and Ruth A. Wallace, *Laity, American and Catholic: Transforming the Church* (Kansas City: Sheed and Ward, 1996), 84.

5. William V. D'Antonio, James D. Davidson, Dean R. Hoge, and Mary L. Gautier, *American Catholics Today: New Realities of Their Faith and Their Church* (Lanham, MD: Rowman and Littlefield, 2007), esp. 17–20.

6. Thomas Zanzig, "Adolescent Confirmation: Gift to the Adult Community," *The Living Light* 28, no. 3 (Spring 1992): 241.

7. See, for example, Steven R. Hemler, "The Case for Adult Confirmation," *Liguorian* 80, no. 6 (June 1992): 22, and John Roberto, "Adolescent Confirmation: Rite of Exit," *The Living Light* 28, no. 3 (Spring 1992).

8. Dan Grippo, "Confirmation: No One Under 18 Need Apply," *U.S. Catholic* 47, no. 8 (August 1982): 32 (emphasis in original). See also Thomas R. Artz, "Confirmation: The Sacrament of Spiritual Maturity," *Liguorian* 69, no. 6 (June 1981), who similarly emphasizes the choice of confirmandi and pushes for later confirmation.

9. See Ambrose of Milan, *De mysteriis* (c. 387), VII.42.

10. See Paul Turner, *Ages of Initiation: The First Two Christian Millennia with CD-ROM of Source Excerpts* (Collegeville, MN: Liturgical Press, 2000), 8, 10, 14.

11. Joseph Moore, *CHOICE: A Two-Year Confirmation Process for Emerging Young Adults* (New York: Paulist Press, 1986), 1.

12. Steven R. Hemler, "The Case for Adult Confirmation," *Modern Liturgy* 16, no. 8 (October 1989): 16–17. Hemler emphasizes the evangelical impulse that O'Brien calls indicative of the culture to which Catholics have adapted.

13. Ibid., 25–26.

14. Brigid M. O'Donnell, "Confirming Young Adults," *The Living Light* 28, no. 3 (Spring 1992): 248.

15. Frank C. Quinn, "Confirmation Is Not Graduation," *Modern Liturgy* 18, no. 7 (September 1991): 11.

16. Ray R. Noll, *Sacraments: A New Understanding for a New Generation* (Mystic, CT: Twenty-Third Publications, 1999), 73, 74.

17. Ibid., 75. Noll says that canon law mandates only that confirmation "should happen at the appropriate time." This is curious. Canon 891 reserves room for national bishops conferences to determine another age if suitable, yet it does establish the "age of discretion" as the universal norm. It reads, "The sacrament of confirmation is to be conferred on the faithful at about the age of discretion unless the conference of bishops has determined another age, or there is danger of death, or in the judgment of the minister a grave cause suggests otherwise." *Code of Canon Law: Latin-English Edition* (Washington, DC: Canon Law Society of America, 1999), 292.

18. Noll, *Sacraments*, 75.

19. Ibid., 173–75.

20. Joseph Martos, *Doors to the Sacred: A Historical Introduction to Sacraments in the Roman Catholic Church*, rev. and updated ed. (Liguori, MO: Triumph, 2001, orig. pub. 1981), 202–3, 206–7.

21. Ibid., 202.

22. *Catechism of the Catholic Church* (New York: Doubleday, 1997), par. 1308. "Although Confirmation is sometimes called the 'sacrament of Christian maturity,' we must not confuse adult faith with the adult age of natural growth, nor forget that the baptismal grace is a grace of free, unmerited election and does not need 'ratification' to become effective."

23. Joseph Martos, "The New Confirmation Debate: Part 1, Posing the Question," *Catechist* 25, no. 6 (March 1992): 19–24, and Martos, "The New Confirmation Debate: Part 2, Resolving the Dilemma," *Catechist* 25, no. 7 (April/May 1992): 56–60.

24. Martos, *Doors to the Sacred*, 116.

25. Bernard Cooke, *Sacraments and Sacramentality*, rev. ed. (Mystic, CT: Twenty-Third Publications, 1994, orig. pub. 1983), 147–48.

26. Paul Lippard, "Is There Life After Confirmation?" *Catechist* 18, no. 5 (January 1985): 38.

27. Frank Sokol, "Confirmation: a Sacrament That Completes or Connects?" *Catechist* 18, no. 5 (January 1985): 32.

28. Thomas Taylor, "Let Them Say 'When,'" *Catechist* 22, no. 5 (January 1989): 14.

29. Lenore L. Danesco, "What Happens After Confirmation?" *Religion Teacher's Journal* 29, no. 8 (February 1996): 12. Paul Turner relays an all-too-ironic pastoral anecdote.

Immediately after the confirmation of a sixteen-year-old, his ten-year-old friend innocently asked, "Does this mean that you don't have to go to church anymore?" While the elder friend responded in the negative, Turner asks the pressing question, "But don't we all wonder?" See "That the Intimate Connection of Confirmation with the Whole of Christian Initiation May Stand Out More Clearly," *National Bulletin on Liturgy* 36, no. 174 (Fall 2003): 150.

30. See also Danesco's later article, "The Call of Confirmation: Helping Children Choose Jesus," *Creative Catechist* 45, no. 1 (January 2011): 12–13.

31. Mary Ann Unkelbach, "Catholic Literacy: A Preparation for Confirmation," *Catechist* 16, no. 6 (February 1983): 36. See also Sue Brown, "A Confirmation Geocache: Locating the Holy Spirit through Technology," *Momentum* 38, no. 3 (September/October 2007): 40–42.

32. United States Conference of Catholic Bishops, Committee on Pastoral Practices, *Receive the Gift, The Age of Confirmation: A Resource Guide for Bishops* (Washington, DC: USCCB Publishing, 2004), 13, 14.

33. Roger Mahony, "Confirmation: Sacrament of Initiation," *Origins* 11 (May 28, 1981): 20–27, esp. 23.

34. William J. Levada, "Reflections of the Age of Confirmation," *Theological Studies* 57 (1996): 310.

35. Margaret Hanrahan, *Celebrating Our Faith*, Catechist Manual (n.p.: Brown-ROA, 2000), 3, see also 93.

36. Sisters of Notre Dame, Chardon, OH, *Confirmed in the Spirit*, Catechist Guide (Chicago: Loyola Press, 2007), xxx.

37. Diocese of Lafayette, Louisiana, Ad Hoc Committee on the Age of Confirmation, "Final Report and Recommendations to the Council of Priests of the Diocese of Lafayette" (April 21, 2005), 38.

38. German Martinez, *Signs of Freedom: Theology of the Christian Sacraments* (New York: Paulist Press, 2003), 125.

39. Paul Turner, "Confirmation: No More Winging It!" *Modern Liturgy* 18, no. 7 (September 1991): 7. Turner's argument that infant baptism comes into question when confirmation is understood as commitment finds verification in Lawler's theology of confirmation in which neither baptism nor confirmation need be celebrated hurriedly in infancy. See Michael G. Lawler, *Symbol and Sacrament: A Contemporary Sacramental Theology* (Omaha: Creighton University Press, 1995), 82–104, esp. 99–101.

40. For the former see, Paul Turner, *The Meaning and Practice of Confirmation: Perspectives from a Sixteenth Century Controversy*, The American University Studies Series VII: Theology and Religion 31 (New York: Peter Lang, 1987); Turner, *Sources of Confirmation: From the Fathers Through the Reformers* (Collegeville, MN: Liturgical Press, 1993); Turner, *Ages of Initiation*.

41. Joseph Gerry, "Confirmation: A Sacrament of Initiation," *Origins* 27 (November 6, 1997): 358–62.

42. Catechists in the diocese of Portland compiled *Celebrating Confirmation Before First Communion: A Resource Kit for Restoring the Order on the Initiation Sacraments*, ed. Michael J. Henchal (San Jose: Resource Publications, 2002). There are also many articles on the topic written by Portland priests and religious educators and published

in catechetical journals. See, for example, Barbara A. Smith, "Confirmation: Sacrament of Initiation or Mature Faith?" *Religion Teacher's Journal* 43, no. 1 (January/February 2010): 14–15, and Marc Caron "The Missionary Nature of Confirmation," *Catechumenate* 31, no. 6 (November 2009): 27–30.

43. John Roberto, *Confirmation in the American Catholic Church* (Washington, DC: National Conference of Diocesan Directors of Religious Education/CCD, 1978), 50.

44. John Roberto, "Adolescent Confirmation: Rite of Exit," *The Living Light* 28, no. 3 (Spring 1992): 247, 246. For an overview of his earlier analysis, see chapter 3.

45. Aidan Kavanagh, *Confirmation: Origins and Reform* (New York: Pueblo, 1988), x.

46. Ibid., 89–96.

47. Ibid., 97.

48. Ibid., 86. Kavanagh thinks even further that the RCIA pushes the church in the welcome direction of wider adult baptism.

49. Aidan Kavanagh, *The Shape of Baptism* (New York: Pueblo, 1978).

50. Ibid., 109.

51. Joseph Martos, "The New Confirmation Debate: Part 1, Posing the Question," *Catechist* 25, no. 6 (March 1992): 22–23.

52. Ibid., 23.

53. Ibid.

54. Joseph Martos, "The New Confirmation Debate: Part 2, Resolving the Dilemma," *Catechist* 25, no. 7 (April/May 1992): 59.

55. Martos, "The New Confirmation Debate: Part 1," 24.

56. Paul Turner, *Ages of Initiation*, 2 (italics in original). Turner has scholarly company in this argument. See, for example, Mark Searle, "Infant Baptism Reconsidered," in *Living Water, Sealing Spirit*, ed. Maxwell Johnson (Collegeville, MN: Liturgical Press, 1995), esp. 368–70.

57. Turner, *Ages of Initiation*, 6.

58. Ibid, 11.

59. Ibid., 30.

60. Ibid, 51–56. Turner identifies fourteen different shapes that the celebration of baptism, confirmation, and Eucharist took historically.

61. Ibid., 63.

62. On the last one see Bishop Alvaro Corrada del Rio's influential pastoral on the topic, "Confirmation, Sacrament of Initiation," *Origins* 35, no. 22 (November 10, 2005): 357–63. Some of the statistics are available in Stella Marie Jeffrey, "Christian Initiation: A Pastoral Perspective on Restored Order," *Antiphon* 9, no. 3 (2005): 245–52. Jeffrey also notes a few dioceses that initiated the baptism-confirmation-Eucharist sequence and then reverted to confirmation after First Eucharist.

63. William J. Freburger, "Confirmation, We Hardly Knew Ye," *The Priest* 48, no. 6 (June 1992): 28. Freburger cites instances of "restoring the order," suggesting that these parishes are indicative of a national trend.

64. Enrico Hernandez, "Restoring the Order of the Sacraments of Initiation for Children Baptized As Infants" (M.A. thesis, Saint Patrick's Seminary, 1997), 33, 50. Canon 891 set the age for confirmation at about the age of discretion unless bishops' conferences determine another age. In 2001, the USCCB set the age of confirmation

between "the age of discretion and about sixteen years of age." USCCB Office of Media Relations, "Age of Confirmation Decreed" (August 31, 2001), http://old.usccb .org/comm/archives/2001/01-150.shtml. See also religious educator Patricia Lawlor's, "Preparing Families to Celebrate Confirmation & Eucharist," *Church* 13, no. 3 (Fall 1997): 25–27, in which she argues for the "restored order," citing the Diocese of Greensburg as an example. Seminarian Kevin M. Lucas also authored an argument for the "restored order": "An Appropriate Age for the Conferral of the Sacrament of Confirmation," *Christ to the World* 51, no. 6 (2006): 529–34.

65. Michael Henchal, "Restoring the Order of the Initiation Sacraments," *Ministry and Liturgy* 29, no. 3 (April 2002): 19.

66. See his Post Synodal Exhortation, *Sacramentum Caritatis* (February 22, 2007), in which the pope emphasized the unity of the sacraments of initiation and specifically that baptism and confirmation are ordered to the Eucharist.

67. See the somewhat misleadingly titled "Bishop Aquila Obtains Papal Approval for Changing Order of Sacraments," *National Catholic Register* (March 9, 2012), http://www.ncregister.com/daily-news/bishop-aquila-obtains-papal -approval-for-changing-order-of-sacraments/.

Chapter 5
A Way Forward for Confirmation?

1. Louis-Marie Chauvet, *Symbol and Sacrament: A Sacramental Reinterpretation of Christian Existence*, trans. Patrick Madigan and Madeleine Beaumont (Collegeville, MN: Liturgical Press, 1995, orig. pub. *Symbole et sacrament: Une relecture sacramentelle de l'existence chrétienne* [Paris: Cerf, 1987]), 414. With these words, Chauvet explicates the association of the sacraments and the church at Vatican II.

2. Yves Congar, *I Believe in the Holy Spirit*, 3 vols., trans. David Smith (New York: Seabury Press, 1983), 1:156.

3. There are many who explore this aspect of American culture, but Roberto Goizueta illustrates the contrast very nicely. See his *Caminemos con Jesus: Toward a Hispanic/ Latino Theology of Accompaniment* (Maryknoll, NY: Orbis Books, 1995).

4. Kimberly Hope Belcher, *Efficacious Engagement: Sacramental Participation in the Trinitarian Mystery* (Collegeville, MN: Liturgical Press, 2011), 125–26.

5. Thomas Aquinas, *Summa Theologiae* III.72.9. ad 1. Thomas uncritically picks up the military imagery surrounding this description of the grace of confirmation, so he describes the grace as "strengthening for combat." I've discussed these military overtones in chapter 1.

6. On the failure of the language of production, in which things and objects are given and taken, for discussing sacramental grace, see Chauvet, *Symbol and Sacrament*, 101–21, esp. 107.

7. Chauvet, *Symbol and Sacrament*, 45. Cf. Exodus 16.

8. Athanasius, *On the Incarnation*, 54, http://www.ccel.org/ccel/athanasius /incarnation.ix.html.

9. M. Therese Lysaught, "Becoming One Body: Healthcare and Cloning," in *The Blackwell Companion to Christian Ethics*, ed. Stanley Hauerwas and Samuel Wells, Blackwell Companions to Religion (Malden, MA: Blackwell Publishing, 2004), 271.

10. Walter Kasper, *The God of Jesus Christ*, trans. Matthew J. O'Connell, with a new foreword by Anthony J. Godzieba (New York: Crossroad, 1984), 206.

11. Gerard Fourez, "Celebrating the Spirit with Adolescents," *The Living Light* 23, no. 3 (March 1987): 201.

12. Ibid., 206, 202.

13. Ibid., 201.

14. Ibid., 203.

15. German Martinez, *Signs of Freedom: Theology of the Christian Sacraments* (New York: Paulist Press, 2003), 6.

16. Ibid., 134.

17. Ibid., 132.

18. Christopher O'Donnell, "The Ecclesial Dimension of Confirmation: A Study in Saint Thomas and in the Revised Rite" (S.T.D. diss., Pontificiae Universitatis Gregorianae, 1987), esp. 115, 123.

19. Ibid., 115.

20. Turner's pastoral sense is palpable. See his *Confirmation: The Baby in Solomon's Court, Revised and Updated* (Chicago: Hillenbrand Books, 2006), where Turner writes, "One should not confuse the printed ritual texts with actual pastoral practice. . . . What the ritual book of any church says is not what actually happens in the sanctuary" (56) and later, "Does confirmation really matter to people? Theologically and canonically, yes it does. Practically, however, it often does not" (84).

21. Ibid., 106.

22. Paul Turner, *Ages of Initiation: The First Two Christian Millennia with CD-ROM of Source Excerpts* (Collegeville, MN: Liturgical Press, 2000), 63.

23. Turner, *Confirmation*, 9.

24. Ibid.

25. Ted Furlow, "Lifelines," *America* 184, no. 3 (February 5, 2001): 26.

26. Ibid.

27. Ibid.

28. Joan Eckstein, "Confirmation: A Problem Sacrament," *Catechist* 20, no. 5 (January 1987): 36.

29. Ibid., 38–41.

30. Ibid., 36.

31. Ibid., 41.

Bibliography

Alma Marie, Sister, and Sister Helen Claire. *Preparing for Confirmation*. On Our Way Series. New York: Sadlier, 1964.

Alonso, Arthur. *Catholic Action and the Laity*. Translated by Cornelius J. Crowley. St. Louis: Herder, 1961.

Amodei, Michael. "I Don't Have to Do Anything?" *Religion Teacher's Journal* 33, no. 7 (January 2000): 12–14.

Antekeier, Charles, Van Vandagriff, and Janet Vandagriff. *Confirmation: The Power of the Spirit, A Charismatic Preparation Program for Youth, Their Parents and Sponsors*. With an introduction by Joseph C. McKinney. Notre Dame: Ave Maria Press, 1972.

Appleby, R. Scott. "The Emergence of the Orchestra Leader, 1973–." In *Transforming Parish Ministry: The Changing Roles of Catholic Clergy, Laity, and Women Religious*, edited by Jay P. Dolan (New York: Crossroad, 1989).

Aquinas, Thomas. *Summa Theologica*. Translated by the Fathers of the English Dominican Province. New York: Benziger Brothers, 1947.

Artz, Thomas R. "Confirmation: The Sacrament of Spiritual Maturity." *Liguorian* 69, no. 6 (June 1981): 34–39.

Auer, Jim. "Confirmation: Clueless No More." *Liguorian* 91, no. 4 (April 2003): 28–30.

Austin, Gerard. "What Has Happened to Confirmation?" *Worship* 50, no. 5 (Summer 1976): 420–26.

Avella, Steven M., with Jeffrey Zalar. "Sanctity in the Era of Catholic Action: The Case of St. Pius X." *U.S. Catholic Historian* 15 (1997): 57–80.

Barger, Robert Newton. "The New Rite of Confirmation." *Worship* 45, no. 9 (November 1971): 566–68.

Beach, Matthew. "Confirmation 'Contract' Demands 'Commitment.'" *National Catholic Reporter* 12 (November 28, 1975): 3.

Bednarski, Gloriani. "A Total Parish Preparation Plan for Confirmation." *Living Light* 9 (Spring 1972): 124–35.

Belcher, Kimberly Hope. *Efficacious Engagement: Sacramental Participation in the Trinitarian Mystery.* Collegeville, MN: Liturgical Press, 2011.

Benedict XVI. Post Synodal Exhortation, *Sacramentum Caritatis,* February 22, 2007.

Bentley, A. "Sacrament of Confirmation: New Decisions and Decrees." *Clergy Review* 10 (1935): 63–65.

Bohen, Marian. *Confirmation: Gift of the Spirit.* The Paulist Press Pamphlet Series. Glen Rock, NJ: Paulist Press, 1962.

———. *The Mystery of Confirmation: A Theology of the Sacrament.* New York: Herder and Herder, 1963.

———. "Confirmation Catechesis." *Worship* 38, no. 11 (January 1964): 84–91.

Brankin, Anthony J. "Confirmation: The Mystical Seal of the Holy Spirit." *Homiletic and Pastoral Review* 80 (April 1980): 11–16.

Braun, Michael, and Doris Murphy. "Profile of a Preparation Program: Confirmation in La Crosse." *Liturgy* 25, no. 1 (January/February 1980): 12–14.

Breckenridge, James F. *The Theological Self-Understanding of the Catholic Charismatic Movement.* Washington, DC: University Press of America, 1980.

Breitenbeck, Gerard. "Should the Retarded Be Confirmed?" *Liguorian* 55 (January 1967): 26–31.

Brown, Sue. "A Confirmation Geocache: Locating the Holy Spirit through Technology." *Momentum* 38, no. 3 (September/October 2007): 40–42.

Bryce, Mary Charles. "Confirmation: Being and Becoming Christian." *Worship* 41, no. 5 (May 1967): 284–98.

Buckley, Francis. "What Age for Confirmation?" *Theological Studies* 27, no. 4 (December 1966): 655–66.

———. "Witness for the Gospel." *The Living Light* 28, no. 3 (Spring 1992): 244–45.

Budzynski, Gerard J. "Making Confirmation a Parish Event." *Catechist* 19, no. 5 (January 1986): 50–51.

Buswell, Charles A. "Pastoral Suggestions for the Celebration of Confirmation." *Worship* 46, no. 1 (January 1972): 30–34.

Byrne, James. *Threshold of God's Promise: An Introduction to the Catholic Pentecostal Movement.* 3d ed. Notre Dame: Ave Maria Press, 1971.

Camelot, Pierre-Thomas. "La théologie de la Confirmation à la lumière des controverses recentes." *La Maison-Dieu* 54 (1958): 79–91.

Campbell, Debra. "The Heyday of Catholic Action and the Lay Apostolate, 1929–1959." In *Transforming Parish Ministry: The Changing Roles of Catholic Clergy, Laity, and Women Religious,* edited by Jay P. Dolan. New York: Crossroad, 1989.

———. "The Laity in the Age of Aggiornamento, 1960–1969." In *Transforming Parish Ministry: The Changing Roles of Catholic Clergy, Laity, and Women Religious,* edited by Jay P. Dolan. New York: Crossroad, 1989.

Carey, Patrick W. *Catholics in America: A History.* Westport, CT: Praeger, 2004.

Carrubba, Sandy. "Confirmation: Becoming Aware of Community." *Today's Catholic Teacher* 13 (March 1980): 20–21.

Catechism of the Catholic Church. New York: Doubleday, 1997.

Champlin, Joseph M. "Age of Confirmation." *The Priest* 62, no. 5 (May 2006): 33, 43.

Chauvet, Louis-Marie. *Symbol and Sacrament: A Sacramental Reinterpretation of Christian Existence.* Translated by Patrick Madigan and Madeleine Beaumont. Collegeville, MN: Liturgical Press, 1995. Originally published as *Symbole et sacrament: Une relecture sacramentelle de l'existence chrétienne* (Paris: Cerf, 1987).

Chrysantha, M. "Becoming Soldiers of Jesus Christ: A Unit for the Upper Grades." *Journal of Religious Education* 2 (1932): 810–29.

Clark, Stephen B. *Confirmation and the Baptism of the Holy Spirit.* Pecos, NM: Dove Publications, 1969.

Coffey, Kathy. "Confirmation: What's a Parent to Do?" *St. Anthony Messenger* 109, no. 12 (May 2002): 24–27.

Coleman, Bill, and Patty Coleman. *My Confirmation Journal,* rev. ed. Mystic, CT: Twenty-Third Publications, 1991.

Collins, Mary. "Who Are the Hearers of the Word?" *Liturgy* 25 (January/February 1980): 5–7, 42.

Collins, Raymond F. "Confirmation: A Theological Overview." *Homiletic and Pastoral Review* 70 (May 1970): 603–9.

Committee for Pastoral Research and Practices of the National Conference of Catholic Bishops. *Statement on Catholic Charismatic Renewal.* Washington, DC: United States Catholic Conference, 1975.

Conaghan, Charles. "The Debate on the Appropriate Age for Confirmation." *Catechist* 19, no. 5 (January 1986): 48–49.

"Confirmation before First Communion." Letter to the editor and response. *The Ecclesiastical Review* 98 (1938): 160–64.

Congar, Yves. *I Believe in the Holy Spirit.* 3 vols. Translated by David Smith (New York: Seabury Press, 1983).

Connizzo, Karen, ed. *Confirmation: Gifted With the Spirit.* Dayton, OH: Pflaum, 2005.

———. *Confirmation: Receiving the Gift of the Spirit.* Dayton, OH: Pflaum, 2005.

Connors, Charles. "Sacrament as Weapon?" *The Homiletic and Pastoral Review* 62, no. 5 (February 1962): 413–18.

Cooke, Bernard J. Introduction to *From Baptism to the Act of Faith.* By Jean Mouroux. Translated by M. Elizabeth and M. Johnice. Boston: Allyn and Bacon, 1964.

———. *Sacraments and Sacramentality.* Rev. ed. Mystic, CT: Twenty-Third Publications, 1994. Originally published in 1983.

Corrada del Rio, Alvaro. "Confirmation, Sacrament of Initiation." *Origins* 35, no. 22 (November 10, 2005): 357–63.

Crehan, Joseph. "Ten Years' Work on Baptism and Confirmation: 1945–55." *Theological Studies* 17 (1956): 494–515.

Cunningham, Joseph L. "Confirmation: Pastoral Letdown." *America* 136 (February 26, 1977): 164–66.

D'Ambrosio, Marcellino. "*Ressourcement* Theology, *Aggiornamento*, and the Hermeneutics of Tradition." *Communio* 18 (Winter 1991): 530–55.

Danesco, Lenore L. "What Happens After Confirmation?" *Religion Teacher's Journal* 29, no. 8 (February 1996): 12–13.

———. "The Call of Confirmation: Helping Children Choose Jesus." *Creative Catechist* 45, no. 1 (January 2011): 12–13.

D'Antonio, William V., James D. Davidson, Dean R. Hoge, and Mary L. Gautier. *American Catholics Today: New Realities of Their Faith and Their Church*. Lanham, MD: Rowman and Littlefield Publishers, 2007.

D'Antonio, William V., James D. Davidson, Dean R. Hoge, and Ruth A. Wallace. *Laity, American and Catholic: Transforming the Church*. Kansas City: Sheed and Ward, 1996.

"Decisions of the Holy See." *Review for Religious* 6 (January 1947): 24–27.

Deedy, John, ed. *The Catholic Church in the Twentieth Century: Renewing and Reimaging the City of God*. Collegeville, MN: Liturgical Press, 2000.

Delcuve, George. "A Necessity for the Normal Efficacy of Religious Education: Confirmation at the Age of Reason." *Lumen Vitae* 5 (1950): 305–32.

———. "Confirmation: Sacrament of the Apostolate?" *Lumen Vitae* 17 (1962): 457–506.

Delea, Michael. "Every Child's Guide to Confirmation." *Liguorian* 61 (March 1973): 44–46.

de Lubac, Henri. *Catholicism: Christ and the Common Destiny of Man*. Translated by Lancelot Sheppard and Elizabeth Englund. San Francisco: Ignatius Press, 1988. Original French, 1947.

Diocese of Lafayette, Louisiana, Ad Hoc Committee on the Age of Confirmation. "Final Report and Recommendations to the Council of Priests of the Diocese of Lafayette." April 21, 2005.

Dix, Karen. "Can Young Children Be Confirmed?" *U.S. Catholic* 72, no. 4 (April 2007): 41.

Dolan, Jay P. "American Catholics in a Changing Society: A Question in Search of an Answer."

———, ed. *Transforming Parish Ministry: The Changing Roles of Catholic Clergy, Laity, and Women Religious*. New York: Crossroad, 1989.

Dresse, John J. "Confirmation of Children: A Sacrament for Adults." *America* 176 (May 10, 1997): 21.

———. "Don't Wait for Confirmation." *U.S. Catholic* 62, no. 12 (December 1997): 21–25.

Dunlap, Judith. "Confirmation: Catechesis for Early Teens." *Church* 13, no. 3 (Fall 1997): 38–40.

Eckstein, Joan. "Confirmation: A Problem Sacrament." *Catechist* 20, no. 5 (January 1987): 34–41.

Ellis, John Tracy. *American Catholicism*. 2nd ed. Studies in American Religion, edited by Daniel J. Boorstin. Chicago: University of Chicago Press, 1969.

Emswiler, James P. "A Letter to a Confirmand." *Catechist* 13 (May 1980): 9.

Fisher, Ralph. *Confirmation: The Forgotten Sacrament*. Notre Dame: Ave Maria Press, 1961.

Fourez, Gerard. "Celebrating the Spirit with Adolescents." *The Living Light* 23, no. 3 (March 1987): 199–206.

Fowler, Martha. *Confirmation and the "Baptism of the Holy Spirit."* Dove Booklet Series. Pecos, NM: Dove Publications, 1969.

Freburger, William J. "Confirmation, We Hardly Knew Ye." *The Priest* 48, no. 6 (June 1992): 28.

Furlow, Ted. "Lifelines." *America* 184, no. 3 (February 5, 2001): 23–26.

Gaupin, Linda. "Now Confirmation Needs Its Own *Quam Singulari*." In *When Should We Confirm? The Order of Initiation*. Chicago: Liturgy Training Publications, 1989.

———. "Confirmation: Age, Sequence, Timing." Interview by *Modern Liturgy*. *Modern Liturgy* 20, no. 5 (June/July 1993): 8–10.

——— and others. *The Spirit Sets Us Free: Confirmation Preparation for Youth*. Sadlier Sacrament Program. New York: Sadlier, 2000.

Gerry, Joseph. "Confirmation: A Sacrament of Initiation." *Origins* 27 (November 6, 1997): 358–62.

Gillis, James R. "The Case for Confirmation." *The Thomist* 10 (1947): 159–84.

Gleason, Philip. "What Made Catholic Identity a Problem?" In *Faith and the Intellectual Life*, edited by James L. Heft. Notre Dame: University of Notre Dame Press, 1996.

Goizueta, Roberto. *Caminemos con Jesus: Toward a Hispanic/Latino Theology of Accompaniment*. Maryknoll, NY: Orbis Books, 1995.

Greeley, Andrew M. "Pop Psychology and the Gospel." *Theology Today* 33, no. 3 (October 1976): 224–31.

Grippo, Dan. "Confirmation: No One Under 18 Need Apply." *U.S. Catholic* 47, no. 8 (August 1982): 31–32.

Groome, Thomas H. *Christian Religious Education: Sharing Our Story and Vision*. San Francisco: Harper and Row, 1980.

Guzie, Tad. "Should We Cancel Confirmation?" *U.S. Catholic* 44, no. 7 (July 1979): 17–23.

Haas, LaVerne. *Personal Pentecost: The Meaning of Confirmation*. St. Meinrad, IN: Abbey Press, 1973.

Haggerty, Brian A. "Building a Catechesis of Confirmation, Part One: Foundation and Structure." *Catechist* 12 (September 1978): 34–35, 60, 73.

———. "Building a Catechesis of Confirmation, Part Two: Strategies and Techniques." *Catechist* 12 (October 1978): 18–19, 27.

Hanrahan, Margaret. *Celebrating Our Faith*. Catechist Manual. N.p.: Brown-ROA, 2000.

Heffern, Rich. "Step in a Process of Faith Initiation." *National Catholic Reporter* 39 (March 22, 2002): 34–36.

Heft, James L., ed. *Faith and the Intellectual Life*. Notre Dame: University of Notre Dame Press, 1996.

Heiberg, Jeanne. "Confirmation and Maturing Catholics." *Catechist* 20, no. 5 (January 1987): 46–48.

Hemler, Steven R. "The Case for Adult Confirmation." *Modern Liturgy* 16, no. 8 (October 1989): 16–19.

———. "The Case for Adult Confirmation." *Liguorian* 80, no. 6 (June 1992): 20–26.

Henchal, Michael. "Restoring the Order of the Initiation Sacraments." *Ministry and Liturgy* 29, no. 3 (April 2002): 17–19.

Henrici, Peter. "A Sacrament of Maturity." *Communio* 25 (1998): 315–23.

Hernandez, Enrico. "Restoring the Order of the Sacraments of Initiation for Children Baptized As Infants." M.A. thesis, Saint Patrick's Seminary, 1997.

Hesburgh, Theodore. "The Relation of the Sacramental Characters of Baptism and Confirmation to the Lay Apostolate." Ph.D. diss., The Catholic University of America, 1946.

Hover, Margot. "Confirmation Marks a Passage to Maturity." *Religion Teacher's Journal* 11 (February 1978): 44–45.

———. "Confirmation: Questions and Perspectives." *Religion Teacher's Journal* 13 (January 1980): 11–12.

Hughes, Kathleen. *Saying Amen: A Mystagogy of Sacrament*. Chicago: Liturgy Training Publications, 1999.

ICEL, National Conference of Catholic Bishops, Committee on the Liturgy. *The Rites of the Catholic Church as Revised by the Second Vatican Ecumenical Council*, study ed. Vol. 1. Collegeville, MN: Liturgical Press, 1990.

John Paul II. *Doninum et Vivificantem: On the Holy Spirit in the Life of the Church and the World*, May 18, 1986. http://www.vatican.va/holy_father/john _paul_ii/encyclicals/documents/hf_jp-ii_enc_18051986.htm (accessed May 15, 2006).

Johnson, Maxwell, ed. *Living Water, Sealing Spirit*. Collegeville, MN: Liturgical Press, 1995.

Kasper, Walter. *The God of Jesus Christ*. Translated by Matthew J. O'Connell. With a new foreword by Anthony J. Godzieba. New York: Crossroad, 1984.

Kavanagh, Aidan. "Adult Initiation: Process and Ritual." *Liturgy* 22, no. 1 (January 1977).

———. "Life-Cycle Events and Civil Ritual." In *Initiation Theology: Addresses of the Fourth Symposium of the Canadian Liturgical Society Held at the University of Manitoba in Winnipeg, 24–27 May 1977*, edited by James Schmeiser. Toronto: The Anglican Book Centre, 1978.

———. *The Shape of Baptism*. New York: Pueblo, 1978.

———. "Confirmation: A Suggestion from Structure." *Worship* 58, no. 5 (September 1984): 386–95.

———. *Confirmation: Origins and Reform*. New York: Pueblo, 1988.

Keaton, Mary Margaret. "Confirmation for the 'Net Generation.'" *Catechist* 36, no. 4 (January 2003): 26–28.

Keifer, Ralph A. "Confirmation and Christian Maturity: The Deeper Issue." *Worship* 46, no. 10 (December 1972): 601–8.

Kelly, Francis D., and Roger Marchand. *Confirmation: Parent and Child*. New York: Sadlier, 1973.

Kenny, J. P. "The Age for Confirmation." *Worship* 35, no. 1 (December 1960): 4–15.

Kichline, Kathleen MacInnis. "Confirmation and the Catholic High School Student." *Catechist* 21, no. 6 (February 1988): 42–43.

Kiesling, Christopher. *Confirmation and Full Life in the Spirit*. Cincinnati: St. Anthony Messenger Press, 1973.

Kinane, J. "Reply to 'A Plea for early Confirmation of Children.'" *The Irish Ecclesiastical Record* 41 (1933): 307–9.

Klejment, Anne. "'Catholic Digest' and the Catholic Revival, 1936–1945." *U.S. Catholic Historian* 21, no. 3 (Summer 2003): 94–95.

Krawczyk, Marilyn Peters. "Confirmation and the Holy Spirit." *Religion Teacher's Journal* 29, no. 7 (January 1996): 26–27.

Kubick, Arthur J., ed. *Confirming the Faith of Adolescents: An Alternative Future for Confirmation*. New York: Paulist Press, 1991.

Lampe, G. W. H. *The Seal of the Spirit*. London: Longmans, 1951.

Larson, James. "The Abandoned Sacrament." *Homiletic and Pastoral Review* 104, no. 2 (November 2003): 46–51.

Lawler, Michael G. *Symbol and Sacrament: A Contemporary Sacramental Theology*. Omaha: Creighton University Press, 1995.

Lawlor, Patricia. "Preparing Families to Celebrate Confirmation and Eucharist." *Church* 13, no. 3 (Fall 1997): 25–27.

Levada, William J. "Reflections of the Age of Confirmation." *Theological Studies* 57 (1996): 302–12.

Liaison Committee of the National Conference of Catholic Bishops with the Catholic Charismatic Renewal. *A Pastoral Statement on the Catholic Charismatic Renewal*. Washington, DC: United States Catholic Conference, 1984.

Ling, Richard. "A Catechist's Vote for Infant Confirmation." *Living Light* 7 (Spring 1970): 42–56.

Lippard, Paul. "Is There Life After Confirmation?" *Catechist* 18, no. 5 (January 1985): 38.

Lucas, Kevin M. "An Appropriate Age for the Conferral of the Sacrament of Confirmation." *Christ to the World* 51, no. 6 (2006): 529–34.

Luebering, Carol. *Your Child's Confirmation: Reflections for Parents on the Sacrament of Christian Identity*. Cincinnati: St. Anthony Messenger Press, 1987.

Luykx, Boniface. "Confirmation Today." *Worship* 33 (1959): 332–47.

———. "On Confirmation." *Homiletic and Pastoral Review* 73 (November 1972): 59–67.

Lysaught, M. Therese. "Becoming One Body: Healthcare and Cloning." In *The Blackwell Companion to Christian Ethics*, edited by Stanley Hauerwas and Samuel Wells. Blackwell Companions to Religion. Malden, MA: Blackwell Publishing, 2004.

Mahony, Roger. "Confirmation: Sacrament of Initiation." *Origins* 11 (May 28, 1981): 20–27.

Martinez, German. *Signs of Freedom: Theology of the Christian Sacraments*. New York: Paulist Press, 2003.

Martos, Joseph. "Confirmation at the Crossroads." *The Living Light* 28, no. 3 (Spring 1992): 225–39.

———. "The New Confirmation Debate: Part 1, Posing the Question." *Catechist* 25, no. 6 (March 1992): 19–24.

———. "The New Confirmation Debate: Part 2, Resolving the Dilemma." *Catechist* 25, no. 7 (April/May 1992): 56–60.

———. *Doors to the Sacred: A Historical Introduction to Sacraments in the Catholic Church.* Rev. and updated ed. Liguori, MO: Triumph, 2001. Originally published in 1981.

———. "Confirmation Last." *Ministry and Liturgy* 29, no. 10 (December 2002/January 2003): 13–14.

Mauck, Marchita B. "Confirmation in Baton Rouge." *Liturgy* 25, no. 1 (January/February 1980): 9–11.

McAuliffe, Clarence. "The Flames of Confirmation." *Review for Religious* 5 (1946): 345–52.

McCulloch, Patricia. "Confirmation: A Rite to Responsibility." *Church* 13, no. 1 (Spring 1997): 27–29.

McKenzie, Terri Monaghan. "Confirmation First." *Ministry and Liturgy* 29, no. 10 (December 2002/January 2003): 12, 15–6.

McPartlan, Paul. "The Holy Spirit and Confirmation: Time to Put Things Right." *Communio* 25 (1998): 303–14.

Meadows, Tony. "It's Time to Rethink Confirmation." *Today's Parish Minister* 41, no. 3 (March 2009): 36–37.

———. "Our Confirmation Requirements are Few." *Today's Parish Minister* 41, no. 4 (April/May 2009): 36–37.

Meath, Gerard. "Sacerdotal Aspects of the Lay Apostolate." *Orate Fratres* 15 (1941): 457–63. Originally published in *New Blackfriars* 19, no. 222 (September 1938): 668–75.

Michel, Virgil. "Confirmation: Our Apathy." *Orate Fratres* 2 (April 1928): 167–71.

———. "Confirmation: Its Divine Powers." *Orate Fratres* 2 (May 1928): 199–204.

———. "Confirmation: Call to Battle." *Orate Fratres* 2 (June 1928): 234–39.

Mick, Lawrence E. "Liturgical Formation for Confirmation." *Today's Parish* 34, no. 1 (January 2002): 23–27.

Mitchell, Joan, Irene O'Neill, and Marsha Allard Sheppleman. "In What Ways Can Christians Count on Me?" *Catechist* 20, no. 5 (January 1987): 49.

———. "Confirmation is a Sacrament of Commitment." *Catechist* 20, no. 5 (January 1987): 59.

Moore, Joseph. *CHOICE: A Two-Year Confirmation Process for Emerging Young Adults.* New York: Paulist Press, 1986.

———. *CHOICE: My Confirmation Journal.* New York: Paulist Press, 1986.

Nolan, Joseph T. "Rethinking Confirmation." *National Catholic Reporter* 8 (December 17, 1971): 8.

Noll, Ray R. *Sacraments: A New Understanding for a New Generation.* Mystic, CT: Twenty-Third Publications, 1999.

O'Brien, David. "Catholic Youth: The Presumed Become the Pursued." In *The Catholic Church in the Twentieth Century: Renewing and Reimaging the City of God*, edited by John Deedy. Collegeville, MN: Liturgical Press, 2000.

O'Connor, Edward D. *The Pentecostal Movement in the Catholic Church.* Notre Dame: Ave Maria Press, 1971.

O'Donnell, Brigid M. "Confirming Young Adults." *The Living Light* 28, no. 3 (Spring 1992): 248–49.

O' Donnell, Christopher. "The Ecclesial Dimension of Confirmation: A Study in Saint Thomas and in the Revised Rite." S.T.D. diss., Pontificiae Universitatis Gregorianae, 1987.

O'Malley, William J. *Sacraments: Rites of Passage.* Allen, TX: Thomas More, 1995.

O'Neill, Colman. "Confirmation: Witness to Christ" *Doctrine and Life* 12 (1962): 335–45.

———. *Meeting Christ in the Sacraments.* Staten Island, Alba House, 1964.

Osborne, Kenan. *The Christian Sacraments of Initiation: Baptism, Confirmation, Eucharist.* New York: Paulist Press, 1987.

———. *Christian Sacraments in a Postmodern World: A Theology for the Third Millennium.* New York: Paulist Press, 1999.

O'Sullivan, Kevin Rodney. "The RCIA Aiding in the Understanding of the Relationship between Baptism and Confirmation." *Catechumenate* 32, no. 3 (May 2010): 10–21.

Overfield, Kay. "Confirmation: Junior High Style." *Religion Teacher's Journal* 7 (January 1974): 14–17.

"Parochus." "A Plea for early Confirmation of Children." *The Irish Ecclesiastical Record* 41 (1933): 307–9.

Pattee, Daniel. "A Catechesis on Baptism and Confirmation." *Homiletic and Pastoral Review* 105, no. 11–12 (August/September 2005): 46–51.

Peters, Marilyn W. "How Adult Patrons Brought New Life to Our Confirmation Program." *Catechist* 18, no. 5 (January 1985): 39.

The Pontifical Council for the Laity, ed. *Rediscovering Confirmation.* Laity Today. Vatican City, 2000.

Portier, William L. "Here Come the Evangelical Catholics." *Communio* 31 (Spring 2004): 35–66.

Pecklers, Keith F. *The Unread Vision: The Liturgical Movement in the United States of America: 1926–1955*. Collegeville, MN: Liturgical Press, 1998.

Power, David. *Sacrament: The Language of God's Giving*. New York: Crossroad, 1999.

Pius X. *Acerbo Nimis: On Teaching Christian Doctrine* 22, April 15, 1905. http:// www.vatican.va/holy_father/pius_x/encyclicals/documents/hf_p-x _enc_15041905_acerbo-nimis_en.html (accessed February 1, 2006).

Pius XI. *Ex Officiosis Litteris: Apostolic Letter to Cardinal Cerejeira Concerning Catholic Action in Portugal. Acta Apostolicae Sedis* 25 (1934): 628–33.

Quinn, Frank C. "Confirmation Reconsidered: Rite and Meaning." *Worship* 59, no. 4 (July 1985): 354–70.

———. "Confirmation Is Not Graduation." *Modern Liturgy* 18, no. 7 (September 1991): 10–11.

Rahner, Karl. *The Church and the Sacraments*. Quaestiones Disputatae Series 9. Translated by W. J. O'Hara. Freiburg: Herder, 1963.

Ranaghan, Kevin and Dorothy. *Catholic Pentecostals*. New York: Paulist Press, 1969.

Ratzinger, Joseph. *The Nature and Mission of Theology: Approaches to Understanding Its Role in the Light of the Present Controversy*. Translated by Adrian Walker. San Francisco: Ignatius Press, 1995.

Reinhold, H. A. "The Sacrament of Responsibility." *The Commonweal* 32 (May 1940): 58–59.

———. "Christian Responsibility." *Orate Fratres* 16 (October 1942): 510–14.

Rickaby, J. "Why Confirm Before Fourteen!" *The Month* 154 (1929): 308–12.

Roberto, John. "Confirmation in the American Catholic Church." *The Living Light* 15 (Summer 1978): 262–79.

———. *Confirmation in the American Catholic Church*. Washington, DC: National Conference of Diocesan Directors of Religious Education/CCD, 1978.

———. "Adolescent Confirmation: Rite of Exit." *The Living Light* 28, no. 3 (Spring 1992): 246–47.

Rogers, Carl R. *On Becoming a Person: A Therapist's View of Psychotherapy*. Boston: Houghton Mifflin, 1961.

Sacred Congregation of the Discipline of the Sacraments. *Quam Singulari: Decree on First Communion*, August 8, 1910. http://www.papalencyclicals.net /Pius10/p10quam.htm (accessed February 7, 2005).

Sacred Congregation for Divine Worship. *Divinae Consortium Naturae: Apostolic Constitution on the Rite of Confirmation*, August 15, 1971.

Sacrosanctum Concilium: The Dogmatic Constitution on the Sacred Liturgy. In *Vatican Council II: The Conciliar and Post Conciliar Documents: Volume 1*. New rev. ed. Edited and translated by Austin Flannery. Northport, NY: Costello Publishing Company, 1996.

Salai, Sean M. "Catechizing the Head and the Heart: An Integrated Model for Confirmation Ministry." *Heythrop Journal* 52 (2011): 569–95.

Sawyer, Kieran. "A Bibliography on Confirmation." *Liturgy* 25, no. 1 (January/February 1980): 33–35.

———. *Confirming Faith: A Faith Development Program Deepening Your Personal Commitment to Jesus and the Church.* Director's Manual. Notre Dame: Ave Maria Press, 1982.

———. "Readiness for Confirmation." *The Living Light* 24, no. 4 (June 1988): 331–39.

———. "Sealed With the Gift of the Spirit." *National Catholic Reporter* 39 (March 22, 2002): 37–39.

Scanlan, Michael. *A Portion of My Spirit: The Catholic Charismatic Renewal.* St. Paul, MN: Carillon Books, 1979.

Schalk, Adolf. "Pius X and the Lay Apostolate." *Priest's Bulletin* 1 (Summer 1954): 8–15.

Schillebeeckx, Edward. *Christ the Sacrament of the Encounter with God.* Translated by Paul Barrett. Franklin, WI: Sheed and Ward, 1963. Originally published as *Christus, Sacrament van de Godsontmoetimg* (Bilthoven: H. Nelissen, 1960).

Schmeiser, James, ed. *Initiation Theology: Addresses of the Fourth Symposium of the Canadian Liturgical Society Held at the University of Manitoba in Winnipeg 24–27 May 1977.* Toronto: The Anglican Book Centre, 1978.

Schmemann, Alexander. *For the Life of the World: Sacraments and Orthodoxy.* New York: St. Vladimir's Seminary Press, 1973.

———. *Of Water and the Spirit: A Liturgical Study of Baptism.* New York: St. Vladimir's Seminary Press, 1974.

Schorsch, Alexander P. "Notes on Theological Accuracy: Confirmation." *Journal of Religious Instruction* 4 (1934): 868–69.

Scott, Macrina. "Confirmation, Pentecost, and Kohlberg." *Catechist* 16, no. 5 (January 1983): 20–22.

Searle, Mark. "Confirmation: The State of the Question." *Church* 1, no. 4 (Winter 1985): 15–22.

———. "Infant Baptism Reconsidered." In *Living Water, Sealing Spirit*, edited by Maxwell Johnson. Collegeville, MN: Liturgical Press, 1995.

Seethaler, Scott. "What Can Adolescents Confirm at Confirmation?" *Catechist* 27, no. 4 (January 1994): 40–41.

Sisters of Notre Dame, Chardon, OH. *Confirmed in the Spirit.* Catechist Guide. Chicago: Loyola Press, 2007.

Smith, Barbara A. "Confirmation: Sacrament of Initiation or Mature Faith?" *Religion Teacher's Journal* 43, no. 1 (January/February 2010): 14–15.

Smith, George D. "Confirmed to Bear Witness." *Worship* 26 (1952): 385–92.

Smits, Kenneth F. "Confirmation Re-examined: An Evolving Theology and Practice." *Worship* 48, no. 1 (January 1974): 21–29.

Sokol, Frank. "Confirmation: a Sacrament That Completes or Connects?" *Catechist* 18, no. 5 (January 1985): 32.

Stasiak, Kurt. *Sacramental Theology: Means of Grace, Ways of Life.* Catholic Basics: A Pastoral Ministry Series, edited by Thomas P. Walters. Chicago: Loyola Press, 2002.

Stegmann, Basil. "Confirmation, the Armor of the Soul." *Orate Fratres* 2 (March 1928): 134–37.

Steinke, Katherin C. "Seventh-Graders Pitch in at Confirmation Day Celebration." *Catechist* 19, no. 5 (January 1986): 52.

Struckhoff, Charlotte. "The Continuing Confirmation Debate: Response to 'The New Confirmation Debate' by Joseph Martos." *Catechist* 26, no.5 (February 1993): 31–32.

Taylor, Thomas. "Let Them Say 'When.' " *Catechist* 22, no. 5 (January 1989): 14–15.

Tormey, John C. "Thanks, We Needed That." *U.S. Catholic* 39, no. 5 (May 1974): 17–22.

Tozzi, Eugene V. "Confirmation: Clarifying the Choices." *Living Light* 11 (Winter 1974): 549–62.

Turner, Paul. *The Meaning and Practice of Confirmation: Perspectives from a Sixteenth Century Controversy.* The American University Studies Series VII: Theology and Religion 31. New York: Peter Lang, 1987.

———. "Confirmation: No More Winging It!" *Modern Liturgy* 18, no. 7 (September 1991): 6–8.

———. "Bishops." *Modern Liturgy* 20, no. 5 (June/July 1993): 6–7.

———. *Sources of Confirmation: From the Fathers Through the Reformers.* Collegeville, MN: Liturgical Press, 1993.

———. "Confusion Over Confirmation." *Worship* 71, no. 6 (November 1997): 537–45.

———. "Eastern Contributions to Confirmation Theology." *Ephrem's Theological Journal* 2, no. 1 (March 1998): 3–7.

———. *Ages of Initiation: The First Two Christian Millennia with CD-ROM of Source Excerpts.* Collegeville, MN: Liturgical Press, 2000.

———. "That the Intimate Connection of Confirmation with the Whole of Christian Initiation May Stand Out More Clearly." *National Bulletin on Liturgy* 36, no. 174 (Fall 2003): 150–54.

———. *Confirmation: The Baby in Solomon's Court, Revised and Updated.* Chicago: Hillenbrand Books, 2006.

———. "Confirming a Lapsed Catholic." *Catechumenate* 30, no. 2 (March 2008): 2–6.

United States Conference of Catholic Bishops, Committee on Pastoral Practices. *Receive the Gift, The Age of Confirmation: A Resource Guide for Bishops.* Washington, DC: USCCB Publishing, 2004.

Unkelbach, Mary Ann. "Catholic Literacy: A Preparation for Confirmation." *Catechist* 16, no. 6 (February 1983): 36–37.

Vaillancourt, Raymond. *Toward a Renewal of Sacramental Theology.* Translated by Matthew J. O'Connell. Collegeville, MN: Liturgical Press, 1979. Originally published as *Vers un renouveau de la théologie sacramentaire* (Montreal: La Corporation des Éditions Fides, 1977).

Washburn, Tom. "A Catechumenal Model for Confirmation." *The Living Light* 38, no. 3 (Spring 2002): 49–60.

Watson, Dorothy. "Confirmation and the Adolescent." *The Furrow* 21 (April 1970): 242–47.

Weber, Gerard P., James J. Killgallon, and M. Michael O'Shaughnessy. *We Grow in God's Family; Preparation for the Celebration of Confirmation.* New York: Benziger, 1969.

———. *Growth in the Spirit: Preparation for the Celebration of Confirmation.* Parent ed. Beverly Hills: Benziger, 1974.

Weiss, Gerald. "Confirmation: A 'Homey' Approach." *Today's Parish* 19, no. 7 (November/December 1987): 18–19.

Wentz, Audrey. "Affirming Confirmation Sponsors." *Catechist* 20, no. 5 (January 1987): 45.

White, Victor. "The Apostolate of the Laity through Catholic Action." *New Blackfriars* 15 (September 1934): 575–82.

Wild, Robert. "Where There's a Will: Charismatic Renewal and a Parish Confirmation Program." *Living Light* 8 (Winter 1971): 121–26.

Wilde, James A., ed. *When Should We Confirm? The Order of Initiation.* Chicago: Liturgy Training Publications, 1989.

Winters, Anne Marie. "The Continuing Confirmation Debate: Response to 'The New Confirmation Debate' by Joseph Martos." *Catechist* 26, no.5 (February 1993): 32–33.

Winzen, Damasus. "Anointed with the Spirit." *Orate Fratres* 20 (June 1946): 337–43.

———. "Anointed with the Spirit (II): The Fruits of Confirmation." *Orate Fratres* 20 (July 1946): 389–97.

Woodward, Kenneth L. "How to Make Confirmation Signify Something." *U.S. Catholic* 41, no. 2 (February 1976): 24–25.

Zanzig, Thomas. "Adolescent Confirmation: Gift to the Adult Community." *The Living Light* 28, no. 3 (Spring 1992): 240–43.